FOOTPATHS
A BRITISH HISTORY

TOM KING

AMBERLEY

To Tom, Dorothea and Matilda

By the same author:
The Southend Story (with Kevin Furbank)
King & Country
Thames Estuary Trail
Thames Estuary Trail (20th anniversary extended edition)

First published 2024

Amberley Publishing
The Hill, Stroud,
Gloucestershire, GL5 4EP

www.amberley-books.com

ISBN: 978 1 3981 1744 0 (print)
ISBN: 978 1 3981 1745 7 (ebook)

British Library Cataloguing in Publication Data.
A catalogue record for this book is available from the British Library.

Typeset in 10pt on 13pt Celeste.
Origination by Amberley Publishing.
Printed in the UK.

Jog on, jog on, the footpath way
And merrily hent [grab] the stile-a.
Your merry heart goes all the way
Your sad tires in a mile-a.

William Shakespeare, *The Winter's Tale*

An ancient country footpath cuts through the back garden of a cottage in rural Kent.

Contents

1

Introduction

A country footpath crosses a stile and curls through the back garden of a cottage, heading for the lane on the far side. The photograph that forms the frontispiece of this book was taken in Kent, but this spot could be almost anywhere in Britain. The scene is unremarkable, and the path is a modest enough presence. Almost lost in the vegetation of the high English summer, it is taken for granted and, quite literally, downtrodden.

Yet this humble strip of dried mud is part of something far grander. The narrow footpath is a phenomenon of history, and the path story is rife with passion. There is nothing ordinary about a British country footpath.

British, though, is the operative term. The British footpath is one of a kind, as distinctive, eccentric and even faintly absurd as red telephone boxes and pub signs. Other countries and continents have their walking trails, purposefully marching between clearly defined

Two iconic items of street furniture, a public footpath sign and a red pillar box, stand side by side in an East Anglian village. Both are unique to the UK.

destinations. This precision stands out, even when the trails are boiled down into symbols. On maps, they appear as clear, no-nonsense lines. But a British Ordnance Survey map looks different. It is overlaid by a fine mesh of random green dotted lines, the likes of which can be found on no other sane work of cartography anywhere else in the world.

At first, this disorganised maze of dots on the map seems to be random. Then gradually, it starts to assemble into something with a sort of logic, and even a purpose of sorts.

This is the British rights of way system, a prosaic term for a unique phenomenon. The ordinary British footpath is used and loved by mass droves of walkers, but it cannot be compared with the formal hiking trails found in more rationally organised land masses. No committee ever sat down and designed our cobweb of paths. The system is typically British inasmuch as it isn't really a system at all. It was never planned to happen, it just happened. Regarded by a tidy mind, local footpaths are the stuff of nightmares.

Regarded by more poetic and romantic temperaments, however, this disorderly layout holds a surefire appeal. Footpaths, British-style, tend to take their time, as if enjoying the scenery of which they are a part. Supposedly intended to convey a foot traveller from point A to point B without losing their way, British footpaths often get lost themselves, instead delivering the walker to point Z. Footpaths also have a habit of popping up where there is not much point in their presence, other than to irritate landowners, and they are often absent from the scene in places where they could really make themselves useful.

Like the fundamentals of the British constitution itself, our rights of way system evolved in an organic, ad hoc way. Recognition and labelling only arrived once it had become an established fact of geography. All in all, it is a charming muddle.

But that muddle is a venerable one, a long time in the making. Our path network is engrained into the landscape, emerging alongside it, as that landscape evolved from an unpeopled, post-Ice Age wilderness, through the hunter-gatherer and agricultural eras, and into the age of industrial civilisation. The paths were already an integral part of the scene, long before anyone ever thought in terms of landscape as a concept. Their curves echo the grander curves of hills and hollows. Their meanders reflect the way they wend respectfully through the patchwork of the English landscape, with its small fields and grid of hedgerows and generous spattering of horse-ponds.

Footpaths have left their own most pronounced mark on the landscape in the shape of the 'holloways', which can be found right across Britain, on all except the hardest terrains. The deep holloways always have a haunted feel, since we know for a fact that they are the result of hundreds of years of human footfall by vanished generations. 'In many places they are reduced 16 or 18 feet beneath the level of the fields,' wrote the eighteenth-century Hampshire naturalist Gilbert White, 'and exhibit very grotesque and wild appearances from the tangled roots that are exhibited among the strata.'[1]

Fittingly for a nation of jumble sales, the footpath system is made up of a grab-bag of oddments, a bit of this and a bit of that. Brits have never liked to throw anything away, and that includes routes. Footpaths are not fussy. The system has absorbed everything from 10,000-year-old animal trails to abandoned railways and tramways; from Roman roads to discontinued coaching turnpikes. Some paths adhere to the routes of long-demolished town walls, tracing the footsteps of medieval night watchmen. Quite a few paths are the one-time main streets of long-lost villages and towns (the silted up port town of Dunwich, Suffolk, for instance). A Somerset path, steeply ascending a hill, is the one that Jack and

An ancient 'holloway' footpath in the West Country, ground out by wagon wheels and hooves down the centuries.

Jill took to fetch a pail of water. There are even one or two paths that were designed to be footpaths and nothing but footpaths. But they are the exception.

Whatever their origin, paths endured as routes used by ordinary countryfolk, even when their original use had become redundant. Nobody thought to file a record of their origins. Generations that made use of the paths were aware only that their right to walk or ride was anciently established. A good example is the defensive communication line set up by King Alfred the Great in what is now Wiltshire. It allowed for fast manoeuvring of men and horses, in the event of a surprise Danish attack. Eventually the excitement died down, and Wessex lapsed into one of the sleepier quarters of Britain. But the military track remained intact down the centuries, as did the name by which it was known locally, 'The Herepath' – the path of the armed host (see Chapter 4).

Usually paths exist for good historic reasons, but not always. Take the tangle of paths in central Dorset, known locally as 'the Blackmoor Maze'. The tracks are ancient, but it is difficult to determine why they exist at all. They served neither village settlements nor farming communities, nor trade routes. The maze revolves in whorls that come from nowhere and don't head anywhere in particular. This pattern, spun from paths, seems to exist purely for its own sake. Its origins are as indecipherable as those of Stonehenge.[2]

The mish-mash process of path evolution has created a unique, mini highway system for the British Isles. But there is another determining factor that sets our paths apart. For these muddy slivers rest on a powerful substratum, one that protects them as rigorously as if they were the Rock of Gibraltar.

Emblems of the Scottish Borders, the 'triplet' peaks of Eildon Hill stand together in isolated splendour.

The track that links the three peaks dates from the first human settlement, around 1000 BC. A study in footpath resilience, it has remained as a public footpath, open to all comers, ever since.

A footpath may be no more than a line of muddy puddles. It may be overgrown to the point where it is impenetrable. It may have been planted over with crops, so that only the gaps in hedges are left to indicate its one-time line of passage. It may not have carried the weight of a rambler for years. It may well have vanished back into the earth totally. Yet, even when invisible, it is still, by definition, a footway, and the way is a legal right. Just in case anyone forgets that fact, it bears a majestic title, enshrined in law. A footpath, just as much as any trunk road, is part of the King's Highway.

As so often, it can take an outsider to recognise the value of such a quirk. Someone like the American diplomat and novelist Nathaniel Hawthorne, for instance. Hawthorne pronounced himself astonished at the status attached to footpaths. 'An American farmer,' Nathaniel Hawthorne wrote, 'would simply plough across any such path.'[3] But in Britain, he noted, with near wonder, these 'little footprints of the centuries' were 'protected by the full and mighty power of the law of the land'.

Only the process of law can remove a footpath. In common with the M25, a right-of-way footpath cannot simply be shut down or built over, even by the most considerable landowner. Property rights mean nothing to a British footpath. Nor can that right of way simply lapse from neglect. This unbending legal principle goes back at least to the year 1315, and the case *Re Inhabitants of St James, Taunton.*[4] It was reiterated, beyond challenge, by *Benn v Hardinge* (2002), in which the court stated that a right of way remained in place, despite evidence that it had not been used for 175 years.

If the British footpath is unique, the same can be said, even more emphatically, about the passions that it has aroused and continues to arouse. The paths never had any conscious archivists, but their history is written in the fervour of those who battled on their behalf. Earth-shaking conflicts (chronicled in Chapter 8) have erupted around these supposedly peaceful presences. On at least one occasion, path passions erupted into murder and death by hanging. The poet and author Robert Graves was a veteran of the bloodiest battles of the Western Front. After the war, he became involved in a footpath dispute centred on his home village, Islip, in Oxfordshire.[5] Nothing he had witnessed on the Somme, Graves averred, could match the level of ferocity unleashed by a bid to close this local right of way.

This book is not about the great, but deliberately planned routes such as the Pennine Way, magnificent though these are (and most of them, anyway, have relied on stitching together existing ancient footpaths, then giving the new trail an impressive title). Deliberately omitted are the Cumbrian fells, the Snowdonia paths, the Scottish wilderness trails and the Lyke Wake Walk across the wild North Yorkshire Moors They have been celebrated enough down the years. Instead, I wanted to tell the story of the everyday footpath, and its quite remarkable, and anything but everyday, history. For the most part, the story draws on the comfortable, unintimidating landscapes of southern Britain. People, not mountains, are the dominant presence. And people have trodden out something that is indeed remarkable. Nowhere is there anything remotely akin to the lovingly preserved, intensively used, obsessively signposted and stiled, diligently monitored, close-knit Lilliputian capillary system that is the British footpath network.

Above all, the paths have always been viewed as a totem of liberty. Paths are great levellers. Baked into every yard of mud is a sense of freedom and equal opportunity, a force so strong that it managed to confound even the Feudal System. People who had little in the way of money or property at least had their rights, and one of these was the right to walk

Path power
in action:
the ancient
brook path
linking the
Essex villages
of Great
Bardfield and
Finchingfield
thrusts its
way through
a gap in a
line of terrace
houses. Built
in the 1890s,
the terrace
had to leave
a gap for the
path, deferring
to the legal
authority of
an ancient
walking route.

freely along old established rights of way. Paths themselves express this sense of freedom by venturing into the most intimate places, often to the vexation of those living there. They can be the bane of those responsible for VIP security. One footpath, finally diverted (despite widespread objection) in 1973, passed within 70 yards of the prime minister's study at Chequers, the premier's country residence. This impudence is another feature of British footpaths which sets them apart. They have a particular liking for getting up close and personal with the country piles of music and film industry moguls, such as Mick Jagger, Andrew Lloyd Webber, Cameron Macintosh, Keith Richards and Stanley Kubrick, all of whom have had run-ins with footpath activists at some stage.

As a result, British footpaths have often found themselves being picked up and flourished as a symbol of democratic values and fair play. Lloyd George recognised and made rhetoric with this when, as Chancellor of the Exchequer, he introduced the 1909 Old Age Pensions Act. In his historic 'Limehouse' address, he pronounced: 'It is rather hard that

A photograph taken *c*. 1900 from an ancient public footpath that ran within a few yards of the prime minister's country residence, Chequers, in Buckinghamshire. It was finally diverted, on security grounds, in 1973 – a rare case of a footpath being closed, in the face of protests, on national and international security grounds.

an old workman should have to find his way to the gates of the tomb bleeding and footsore through the brambles and thorns of poverty. We cut a new path for him ... through fields of waving corn.'

Paths certainly have their use as metaphors like this, but for the most part they are a grounded affair, literally, not just metaphorically. They have come into being because of practical requirements. They serve the needs of human work and the cravings of leisure.

Yet, fancy also tends to creep into the mix. It can be hard to escape the feeling that paths are living things, animal rather than vegetable and mineral. There is undoubtedly something ethereal about them as well. In the old countryside there was a widespread belief in fairy paths. These might be regular rights of way during the daytime. But they should never be followed at night time, when they became the fairies' domain. The word bewildered entered the language as a result of fairy-path lore. It applied to a traveller, or lover, who had been led astray along a pixie path, eventually to emerge a strange and transformed person, one who had been wilded in the other world of fairyland.

And the fairies are still at work. Be warned by one who has been thus bewitched by the British rights of way system, and carries the wild look in his eye to show for it. It is many years now since this author's country rambles ceased to focus on the next horizon, and instead concentrated on the magic ribbon at foot level. Keep your eyes on the horizon. Fixate on the next objective. Don't look down for too long. For if you do, the footpath will start to exert its grip, and although that path may carry you to where you want to go, you will still be lost.

As the moon emerges, a path through the woods is transformed into a line of dancing fairies. Old country folk knew better than to venture on such paths by night. From a painting by Arthur Rackham.

Gateway to the beyond: a stile in Somerset beckons walkers over the hills and far away.

2

Ancient Origins:
Animal Tracks

The oldest footpaths in the British Isles weren't formed by feet at all, but by paws and hooves. Many of the paths still walked today were trodden out by animals, 10,000 years ago. Four-legged beasts were the first trailblazers, engineering routes through the land as the Ice Age receded and fertility returned. Only much later did *Homo erectus* move in with possession orders, after letting feral beasts do the work.

Animals stick to the same tracks forged by their ancestors for generation after generation. The soldier and scholar T. E. Lawrence, famous for his First World War exploits as 'Lawrence of Arabia', observed this phenomenon in camels.[1] As they made their way through the desert. the animals undeviatingly followed ancient camel paths. These were ways, scored into the desert across apparently featureless sands, that were wholly invisible to the man mounted on the camel's back.

All this can be said with confidence, although, of course, clear identification of ancient animal tracks is not easy. There were no human witnesses to their creation. Animals didn't litter their tracks with archaeologically useful flints and bits of broken pottery. But there are clues. Look for a path that moves in a series of ambling, leisurely curves; has been trodden into a hollow by constant usage; and descends from high, dry, ground to a river or other watering place.

One clear example survives at Northward Hill, in Kent, overlooking the Thames Estuary. The path twists through ancient woodland on rough virgin land that has never been developed for agriculture. The path bears all the telltale signs of an ancient animal track, along with an additional prehistoric resonance. Below the hill lies a wide expanse of marshland, leading almost uninterrupted upriver to Swanscombe. It was here, in 1935, that Britain's oldest human remains were disinterred. The skull parts belonged to 'Swanscombe Woman', who lived and died in these fertile marshes 400,000 years ago. For humans and paths alike, the Thames Estuary marshes were a nursery.

Landscape historians also benefit from the assistance of a most useful field worker. The badger is thought to have been the first mammal to colonise the British Isles after the Ice Age. The poet Edward Thomas refers to *Meles meles* as 'the most ancient Briton'.[2]

An ancient animal-forged path from the top of Northward Hill, Kent, at the point where it descends to the Thames marshes below.

Badgers are tenacious creatures of habit. They sniff their way along the same ancestral foraging trails, night after night, year after year, century after century, never deviating. Ancient badger trails are imprinted into the boulder clay ridges and gravel banks along the north shore of the Thames Estuary. Most of these are now established rights of way for humans, but at night the badgers return, as they have for perhaps 10,000 years. In some places, such as Thundersley Glen and Vange, houses have been built, most unwisely, across these ancient tracks. Badgers continue to burrow their way, relentlessly, under the properties. The author talked to one homeowner who gave up the struggle. 'I just open my front door and my back door and let them pass through from one side to the other.'

Creature of habit: Snow lies thick on the ground, but a badger still elects to follow the ancient track, trodden out by its ancestors over millennia. A scraper-board illustration, captured from life in Bearshanks Wood, Northamptonshire, by the artist and writer D. J. Watkins-Pitchford.

Human witnesses did get one glimpse into animal trailblazing at first hand. It happened when Europeans started to colonise North America. Early settlers found themselves in a vast primeval forest. It was a whole new experience for West Europeans, whose settled rural environments consisted of orderly fields, woods, orchards and heaths. For decades, the forest-clad mountains of Appalachia proved a formidable barrier to expansion. However, backwoodsmen like the legendary Daniel Boone observed how the movement of herds of buffalo had beaten even the mountains, as they trampled out routes into their winter feeding grounds in the Mississippi basin. Native Americana borrowed these routes for part of the year, while giving them a wide berth at mass migration time. Long after the mountain trail had been officially dubbed the Cumberland Gap (after the Duke of Cumberland, victor at Culloden), it was known locally as the Buffalo Trace. It was along this animal trail that Daniel Boone led thousands of westward settlers.

Another buffalo-forged 'trace' was known as the Wecquaesgeek Trail. It ran from the southern tip of Manhattan, forming a spine down the centre of the island, before heading up the east bank of the Hudson River. It was adopted by Dutch settlers, and in course of time became New York City's most famous thoroughfare. In highway terms, Broadway is about as far from a footpath as it is possible to get, yet its trajectory and its dimensions owe everything to animal pathfinders. Whether badgers or buffalo, the animals have received little thanks for their role.

Frontiersman Daniel Boone leads one of many settler parties through the Cumberland Gap, on to the great prairies that lay beyond. The animal bones on the ground testify to the mass movement of buffalo and elk that took place annually, and which established the trail in the first place. The painting, by John Caleb Bingham, dates from 1850, by which time both Daniel Boone and the Cumberland Gap were legendary names in American history. By then, the herds of buffalo responsible for the path were all but extinct.

3

Ancient Origins:
Humans Stride Out

Around 4500 BC, humans began to construct pathways, rather than adopting the ones obligingly provided by animals. In the West of England, this prehistoric generation left behind a stupendous legacy. This was nothing less than the oldest surviving path or road surface in the world (by contrast, the oldest Roman road surface, a mere youngster, dates from around 100 BC).

The Sweet Track, discovered during peat digging in 1970, consisted of oak planks, laid onto cross-beam posts, driven into marshy soil. It allowed for swift traverse across the wetlands now known as the Somerset Levels, and was part of an interlinked communications system between the local 'lake villages'. Wooden paths like the Sweet Track served an almost amphibians race. They allowed these folk to flit around the marshes, oblivious to the treacherous mud. No wading was required.

The Sweet, and its companion tracks, were surveyed and constructed long before the invention of the wheel. As such, they provided an early flourish of the path network that would one day cover every county in England. Other sections continue to be unearthed.

The lake-village tracks provide a fascinating study of the very earliest path construction, but by their very nature they were limited in range. Not much younger are the ridgeways, which by around 3000 BC provided a comprehensive long-distance system of tracks across much of southern England and the Welsh borderlands, from modern-day Dorset to modern-day Norfolk and Shropshire. Clear streaks blazed across the green of the hills, the ridgeways drove confidently along the ridges which gave them their name, lapping up mile after mile, and always on the most commanding high ground. They adhere to the most basic principle of road engineering: economy of purpose. In the word of Alfred Watkins, they are there to 'provide easy travelling'.[1] Direction of travel remains crystal clear because they use the line of the hills as their guide.

The ridgeways heaved with traffic, hundreds of years before the Roman conquest. The Neolithic Age and Bronze Age are sometimes misrepresented. The notion of a few huddled, inward-looking communities, clinging close to their home patch, never venturing beyond the nearest safe horizon, is misleading. The people of the Neolithic era ranged freely and

A replica section of the wooden Sweet Way at the Shapwick Heath nature reserve, on the Somerset Levels. Discovered in 1970, and named after the peat-digger who unearthed it, the Sweet Way is the oldest surviving human path or road surface in the world. The reconstruction follows the line of the original track, now preserved in Taunton Museum.

The Great Ridgeway: The ancient track rolls in rhythm with the rolling Berkshire Downs. In one direction lies the Channel, in the other the Goring Gap, where it crosses the River Thames to join another ancient trackway, the Icknield Way. (From a painting by David Gentleman in the Shell Archive)

quite fast across the island of Britain when they needed to. They were able to do so thanks to their network of, mostly hilltop, long-distance ways. Trade, in livestock and tools, was what propelled them. The evidence lies in the litter of flint axe-heads and other implements scattered along the ridgeways.

Today, these ancient tracks, completely unaltered, provide hundreds of miles of easy rambling routes, linking the Wessex Hills with the upper Thames Valley. On reaching the Chiltern Hills, the chalkland ridgeways then adopt a new name, the Icknield Way. Icknield in its turn descends onto the Anglian flatlands, offering an elevated, inland and still 'easy' passage from the Channel to the North Sea. Further north, the Portway follows an age-old trading route from Wales to northern England along the crest of that long, freakish hill, the Wrekin. In the south-east, a ridgeway follows the entire west–east run of the North Downs, converging on Canterbury. (It has been dubbed, romantically, the Pilgrims' Way, although any sensible pilgrims, including Chaucer's motley bunch, would simply have taken the old Roman road, Watling Street.)

Along the way, the ridgeways offer a surefire route into some of the most spectacular scenery in southern and eastern England. They also serve to link many of Britain's most ancient monuments and archaeological sites, including the Avebury stone circle, the Uffington white horse, and the Grime's Graves flint mines, all adding up to a Cook's tour of the pre-Roman era.

The Peddars Way, running north through Norfolk and Suffolk, isn't a ridgeway, but it is both an ancient highway and an ancient low way. Low, because of the low-lying, flat Anglian countryside that it traverses, high because of its importance as a traffic artery

A drover herds sheep on the Icknield Way, as his forbears had done along the same route for centuries. (Drawing by A. L. Collins, 1916)

Robin Hoods Butts at Alton were used for target practice.

Lord Howard of Effingham, victor over the Armada, is buried at Reigate.

Queen Elizabeth, Izaac Walton, Cobbett and Swift. Farnham Associations.

Prehistoric camp at Oldbury Hill. Roman Villa remains, Titsey Park.

King's Head, Dorking (Dickens' Marquis of Granby) Tony Weller ducked Mr. Stiggins in the horse trough.

STONEHENGE

TITSEY PARK

HOG'S BACK   GUILDFORD
DORKING   COLLEY HILL
FARNHAM   WESTERHAM
ALTON   HOLYBOURNE   ALBURY   OXTED   MAIDSTONE   CANTERBURY
WINCHESTER   REIGATE   HOLLINGBOURNE   CHILHAM
ALRESFORD   LENHAM
EASTON   CHARING
ST CATHERINE'S HILL

Wolfe and Thackeray associations at Westerham.

Colley Hill

Farnham and Guildford road rebuilt by Romans.

Chilham, scene of battle during Roman invasion

John Evelyn, diarist and gardener, lived at Wotton near Albury.

The Canterbury Pilgrims from Chaucer's "Canterbury Tale".

St. Catherine's Hill, famous for its fairs through the centuries.

The Pilgrims' Way

Defeated Royalists set fire to Alresford A.1718.

Murder of Thomas à Becket at Canterbury.

Running west–east along the crest of the Hampshire and North Kent Downs, the Pilgrims' Way connects the cathedral cities of Winchester and Canterbury. It wasn't pilgrims who blazed the way, however. The ancient track predates the Christian era by as much as a millennium. (*c.* 1930, artist unknown)

Peddars Way
Public Footpath
Holme-next-the-Sea
46 miles (74 km)

Angles Way
Public Byway
Thetford
15 miles (24 km)

Angles Way
Great Yarmouth
77 miles (124 km)

Icknield Way
Ivinghoe Beacon
105 miles (169 km)

The meeting point of the Peddars Way and the Icknield Way, at Knettishall Heath, Suffolk. This is a pivotal node in a system of trackways that marches through nine counties, from The Wash to the Channel.

before and during the Roman invasion and occupation of Britannia. It may well be as old as the ridgeways, and it is certainly part of the ancient, pre-Roman transport connection between the Channel and the North Sea. More than just a trade route, it formed a unifying link between the various Iron Age tribes of East Anglia. The Peddars Way may well have been a key factor in military operations, allowing as it did for swift marshalling and movement of forces. Queen Boadicea's violent revolt against the Romans in AD 47 was notable for the speed and suddenness with which she descended on Roman London. The Peddars Way provided a ready springboard for this brutal onslaught. Like the ridgeways, it has now found a more peaceful identity as a 46-mile-long distance footpath. The ultimate tribute came from the Romans themselves. Rather than build their own road across East Anglia, they simply appropriated the Peddars Way for their own uses.

Of course, industry and townships tend to cluster around major highways. The Peddars Way was no exception. East Anglia had a ready-made industry to hand which encouraged early development. Flint tools from the area were exported all over Europe. Prosperity and

A section of the 1:50 000 Ordnance Survey map covering the landscape immediately to the south of Sheringham, Norfolk. Meandering ribbons of yellow capture patterns of tracks laid down during the millennium 500 BC to AD 500, as East Anglia was developed for farming. The ancient ways connect the various hamlets and farmsteads in an intricate mesh. Some of these deep rural tracks have been adopted for use by motor traffic, but many others survive simply as footpaths.

population growth followed. This is one of the first areas where the familiar pattern of English village communities grew up. The flint mines eventually became redundant, but the villages remained (only now most of their populations were engaged in agriculture). The villages were connected by tracks to other villages. Village A might have four tracks branching out from its centre, leading to villages B, C, D and E. Village B would have its own direct connection to village D, and so on. The result is a honeycomb of twisting country lanes. Unlike the Peddars Way, and unlike the later Roman roads, these tracks were never predominantly straight. They moved in comfortable bends and curves, taking their time, and in the process they laid down a latticework pattern of byways across modern-day Norfolk, Suffolk and north Essex. Sometimes these connections double up, so that two neighbouring villages are connected by more than one lane. It is anybody's guess what lies behind this duplication.

There these late Neolithic and Iron Age trackways remain. For the most part they have become macadamised country lanes, but quite a few were never developed for modern traffic. Instead, they dwindled into footpath and bridleway. The network was further developed in the Saxon era. But the first generation of Anglian trackways are contemporary with the ridgeways. They offer a short-distance, less dramatic and lowland alternative for those in search of a prehistoric walk. Wherever you walk in this honeycomb of green lanes, there is a sense of moving through an old, old land.

4

Conflict and Colonisation

Britain's Roman roads proved to have a lot more staying power than the Romans themselves. Over 10,000 miles of hard-paved road were laid down in Britain between the Roman conquest of 43 BC and the Romans' departure in AD 410. The bulk of these routes remain, in one guise or another.

Britain's *Viae Romanae* conformed to a specification laid down by imperial statute and applied right across the Roman Empire. They had to be exactly 12 Roman feet (*pedes*, at 11.65 inches, almost identical to the standard British 1 foot measurement) wide, and constructed on precise templates regarding drainage (*agger*), foundations (*audites*) and top dressing (*statumen*). Building materials varied according to what was locally available, but were always deployed in the same way, according to the same challenges of wear and tear. Where feasible, the roads remained straight, but this was never a *sine qua non*. Occasionally, they would curve or turn in response to landscape and ground conditions. But they never meandered. Above all, they were purposeful.

After the departure of the legions, most Roman constructions, including the entirety of London, withered, decayed and disappeared. This included roads, or to be more exact, road surfaces. The Romans had taken their road-building expertise with them. No further dedicated road construction was undertaken until the advent of the turnpike trusts in the 1660s. The imperial infrastructure dwindled and decayed. The roads in particular were treated as convenient quarries. Surface stones were stripped and used for other purposes. Numerous cottages, barns and stone walls, still standing, are constructed, or partly constructed, from bits of Ermine Street and Akeman Street. But some stretches of hard surface survived. Two Roman roads, in Essex/Hertfordshire and Sussex, even acquired the Saxon name Stane (Stone) in acknowledgement of their paved surfaces, such a contrast to all the other muddy roads. The main trans-national roads, such as Watling Street (London–Dover) or the Great North Road, did remain relatively intact. Indeed, a statute of Edward the Confessor's reign put three of the chief strategic routes – Ermine Street, Watling Street and the Fosse Way – 'under the King's protection'. In the course of time, these undeviating highways become the basis of modern motor roads, the A1, the A2, the A4 and the A5 among them. But the lesser routes, the B roads of Rome, sank back into the countryside. Grass and weeds spread where once there had been hard roadstone.

The weeds marched in parallel with the human barbarians, whose smash-and-grab raids were destroying what remained of the Roman legacy. In time, many old Roman ways were ploughed or planted over.

Yet, in one way, these minor Roman roads were to prove more resilient than the great cross-country highways. Barely a trace remains of the Great North Road or Watling Street, other than their surveyed routes. They have been covered with roadstone and concrete, and widened, in some cases into six-lane motorways.

Roman footpaths, by contrast, would look familiar to ancient Romans, even if shorn of their hard surface. Shreds and short stretches of one-time Roman road lie scattered across the land like twigs on a woodland floor. Along with their survival goes the right to walk along them.

This enduring right of way is a further legacy of imperial Rome.[1] Footpaths being part of the King's Highway (see Introduction), they are protected and championed by the full weight of the law. This legal sacrosanctness springs directly from the statutes of ancient Rome. The Romans valued paths, they cherished rights of passage and they laid down strict rules to prevent both these things being eroded. A transgressor would swiftly find himself in court. Among the titles carried by legal dignitaries was that of Commissioner of Footpaths. This office was also conferred as an honorary award on some non-lawyers. One Roman invested with that weighty title was Julius Caesar.

The *Jus Eundi* (Right of Going) laws established a right of foot passage along an established path even when that path crossed private land. This was the *Jus Ambulandi*, a *jus* that runs through social history and through the pages of this book. In Britain, the Romans may have shut the departure gate behind them, but the *Jus Ambulandi* stayed in place, unfazed by the anarchy of the dark centuries that followed, still legally valid among the ruins. Rights of way law, applied time and again in the British courts, remains in essence Roman law.

On the ground, away from the law books, Roman highways continue to enjoy a lively existence. Their surviving physical form varies from muddy tracks to city high streets. In some cases, they rattle from one manifestation to another with rapidity, ensuring that country ramblers need to stay alert or they will find themselves blocking up the traffic. A good example of a multifaceted Roman road is offered by the Fosse Way. This imperial highway ran north–east from Exeter to Lincoln, passing through Bath, Cirencester and Leicester. Its 230-mile trajectory is still for the most part physically intact today, bisecting middle and southern England. In its passage it ranges from long expanses of hedge-lined rural footpaths and country lanes to busy intercity roads (the A46 Leicester–Lincoln road and the A303 through part of Somerset) and thronged shopping streets in towns and cities along the way. Switches in fortune continue to take place. One stretch, north of Ilchester, was for many years incorporated into the A37. Following construction of a bypass, it has reverted once again to footpath status. If anything, in twenty-first-century Britain, the percentage of this ancient Roman highway going to grass is on the increase.

On the other side of England, Stane Street provides another example of a multiple-personality route. Much of its Roman progress from Chichester to London is now colonised by busy four- or six-lane roads, notably the A3 and A24. Dorking's high street may also be a Stane Street legacy. But elsewhere the Roman highway has reverted to lengths of quiet country bridleways, almost equally busy with walkers and horse riders.

The Fosse Way, near Malmesbury, Wiltshire. Much of the once-mighty Roman highway survives intact in one form or another, ranging from modern A road to country footpath. David Gentleman's painting depicts a point where the Fosse Way switches from a stretch accessible only to walkers and horse riders into a metalled country lane. (Painting by David Gentleman, courtesy of the Shell Archive)

Elsewhere, we find sections adopted as parkland walks. A fine example is the section of almost perfectly preserved Roman road that runs for about 1.5 miles on the west edge of Sutton Park, in the West Midlands. This specimen is part of Ryknield Street, a 275-mile highway that ran from Bourton in Gloucestershire to Templeborough in Yorkshire. Most of Ryknield Street vanished after the Roman evacuation. First it was ploughed up for agricultural purposes, then, in the nineteenth century, remaining vestiges were smothered by the growth of the Birmingham conurbation. Nobody cared about Ryknield Street. In the hierarchy of Roman roads, it had just been a service road, devoid of the strategic importance of the great cross-country highways. But a stretch of it survived thanks to the creation of Sutton Park as a deer-hunting preserve in 1126. The effect was to preserve the entire landscape, Roman road included, as if in amber. In the nineteenth century, the park was steadily transformed into a leisure facility for the enjoyment of Brummies, and the old Roman road became a visitor attraction in its own right. Now, as a footpath, it remains a museum piece of Roman road construction, complete with anger, ditch, classic dimensions and the familiar Roman straightness.

Two of the grandest landscape parks, Blenheim and Stowe, also pay their respects to a Roman road, in this case Akeman Street. At Blenheim the road turned footpath marches north across a field in typically imperious fashion, until it collides with an equally imperious wall. This is the Duke of Marlborough's estate wall, built to define the borders of the great duke's fiefdom, and bar access to those who lacked an invitation. But it can't bar Akeman Street. Blenheim Palace was built at the state's expense in grateful thanks for Marlborough's military victories. But neither state nor duke could buck the *Jus Ambulandi*. So ramblers along the footpath simply cross the wall via a ladder stile, then continue along old Akeman Street, through the park, leaving via a gap in the wall on the far side.

North-east of Blenheim, Akeman Street, now a green lane, forms the eastern boundary of another great landscape park: Stowe. It provides glimpses of some of the temples and follies, honouring the high classical culture and philosophy of Roman civilisation, partly made possible by roads like Akeman Street. But the landscape architect William Kent

Ryknield Street, a Roman military road, has been adopted to form a path through Sutton Park, Sutton Coldfield, the largest public park in the West Midlands.

Roman Akeman Street, intact in the form of a footpath, at the point where it crosses into the grounds of Blenheim Palace, via a ladder stile.

also paid tribute to a different, more practical, aspect of Roman civilisation. As it passes through the landscape park, Akeman Street is incorporated as a carefully preserved feature, and a useful one. As part of the circular route round the park, it continues to function as a thoroughfare.

Similar, if less cosseted, examples can be found across the land. Wherever there were Romans, there were Roman roads, and wherever there were Roman roads, there are likely to be Roman footpaths. Roman footpaths make no attempt to hide their identity. The stone surfaces may be long gone, but these particular paths will be relatively firm underfoot, even at a time when winter conditions have reduced neighbouring footpaths to deep mud. Below ground level the 2000-year-old foundations generally remain intact, incorporated into the local geological structures, and still doing their job. Ever reliable with regard to accurate dimensions, the Roman footpaths will be 16 feet wide, give or take a Roman inch. They will also, of course, in almost all cases, be straight. These are little footpaths with big attitude, following their chosen orientation through thick and thin, as if the Roman Empire was still projecting its will through Europe. Here lies another contrast with other ancient footpaths, which meander as a way of life. Whatever their origins, nowhere else are footpaths so predictable. For all their stern engineering, that feature sets the paths of the Romans apart. Ironically, they number among the oddballs of the footpath system.

Highways were not the only source of modern-day footpaths bequeathed by Rome. Way to the north lurk two more examples of Roman engineering that remain even more impressive than the road network. Antonine's Wall stretched for 39 miles between the Firth of Forth and the River Clyde in central Scotland. Built around AD 140, it marked the northernmost point to which the great Roman Empire ever reached. In every respect, bar one, it is a study in failure. Antonine's Wall was constructed twenty years after the completion of Hadrian's Wall, as part of a military attempt to thrust further north into

Antonine's Wall, near Falkirk, in the Central Lowlands of Scotland. The giant defensive line of turf rampart and ditch marks the northernmost point ever reached by the Roman Empire. Part of the military road, built to service the defences, survives as a footpath.

Caledonia. The so-called 'wall' was in fact a turf bank, around 10 feet high, with a ditch on the northern side. Too feeble for the task entrusted to it, Antonine's Wall was abandoned almost as soon as it was finished. Pushed back by the natives, the Romans retreated to the more formidable defensible line of Hadrian's Wall. Further failure, this time of the landscape variety, followed. The turf wall crumbled away over time. The remnants are sections of ditch, along with one other presence. True to a process that occurs so frequently in the footpath story, the rights of way remain along many sections. Otherwise forgotten, Antonine's Wall survives most effectively as a footpath system.

The same story of footpath survival applies to the more famous Hadrian's Wall. After the departure of the Romans, the wall began a long process of attrition. Nature began to undo it. Local people quarried the wall for stone to build homes and barns. Nothing, however, undermined the wall's role as a thoroughfare. The top level of Hadrian's great monument was eventually reduced to a height just a few feet above ground. Yet, whatever other roles it had relinquished, it remained as a footpath. As late as the mid-1970s, walkers enjoyed the right to stride along the stones, treating them like any other road surface. The route has now been shifted a few (Roman) feet sideways and downwards, so that long-distance walkers proceed alongside the wall rather than on top of it. But they still follow a right of way originally forged by Roman sandals.

It remains infra dig among historians to refer to the immediate post-Roman period as the Dark Ages. Nevertheless, the myths and mysticism that swirl around these centuries tell their own tale. Arthurian and other mythology looks like nothing so much as compensation for the absence of written records and hard facts.

Hadrian's Wall, c. 1920. As late as the 1970s, the wall itself acted as a right of way. Hikers were able to treat the structure itself as a well-paved public footpath.

The conflict of academic theories echoes the confusion of territorial tussles that swirled through the years between the departure of the Romans and the kingship of Alfred the Great. Civilisational conflicts raged across the British Isles. Kingdoms rose and waned. One hard fact, though, is for sure. The huge defensive earthworks, the 'dykes' and 'ditches' that were thrown up during this period, don't lie. They tell their own story of conflict and warring petty kingdoms, of the ebb and flow of territorial boundaries, of the constant apprehension of attack. Dark those centuries may have been, but they were never dull.

The sheer abundance of these dykes and ditches around the British Isles is impressive, as is the scale of labour that must have gone into piling up all that earth. And they were built to last. Among the most formidable survivors are the Devil's Dyke and Fleam Dyke in Cambridgeshire. Across the Chiltern Hills lies a whole series of earthworks, known collectively as the Grim Ditches. In Oxfordshire there is the Wattle Bank (also known as Aves Ditch). Offa's Dyke, running along the Anglo-Welsh border, offers a handy abbreviation for the division between the two home nations. In Wessex, wise King Alfred didn't attempt to build an extravagant earthwork, but utilised the existing ridge between Avebury and Marlborough to create a fortified military track, the Herepath, along which he could move his forces swiftly and decisively.

While we know the purpose of Hadrian's and Antonine's walls, the story of the Dark Age ramparts remains murkier. There is not always a clear reason for their construction. They may have been defensive. They may have been boundary lines. They may simply have been built to impress. Or all three.

The Herepath, near Avebury, Wiltshire. The existing track was upgraded on the instructions of Alfred the Great in order to move forces swiftly along a south-facing defensive line on the Wessex Downs.

What are we to make, for instance, of Cambridgeshire's Devil's Dyke? It is not quite 7 miles long (providing a grandstand view of Newmarket racetrack on the way), 60 feet in height and 120 feet across. It is easy to see how it acquired its name. Only the devil would have had the arrogance to construct such a thing, or the power to requisition sufficient numbers of labourers, drawn from the legion of the damned, to get it built. It always seems to have been there. The Anglo-Saxon Chronicle of 905 calls it The Dyke, on the assumption that everyone knows what it is and where it stands. As a boundary, it neatly defines the border line between the wet fens and the dry chalk country, a differentiation which, to this day, marks Cambridgeshire as a split-personality county. As for its purpose, who can say? Except that it does have an undoubted purpose. A footpath, as old as the earthwork itself, runs along the top of it. On any day, the path is festooned with walkers, many from the nearby university city. It is said that the scientists Crick and Watson, discoverers of the DNA double-helix, took bracing walks along the Devil's Dyke, while they wrestled with a mystery even greater than the dyke itself, the secret of life. Science, combined perhaps with the ancient devilry of The Dyke, duly uncorked the secret.

Massive labour clearly went into the construction of all these great earth ramparts and sinister hollows (the discovery of skulls in the Aves Ditch suggests it may have been the site of ritual executions). The effort was to a large extent wasted. The consolidation of England and Wales into a single, far from petty kingdom rendered the dykes and ditches redundant,

The Devil's Dyke, Cambridgeshire, pictured in 1853.

except perhaps in one respect. The travel writer Bill Bryson walked the full length of the Devil's Dyke. He concluded that the dyke could have had no practical value, 'except to show people in the fen country what it felt like to be 60 feet high'.[2]

Once again, the power that outlasted and superseded all the other powers was path power. Long after the military purpose of these paths had been forgotten, the right to use them as trackways remained, unchallenged by any armed foes.

The earthworks also became redundant in technological terms, as defensive warfare moved into a new era of stone castles and town walls. Across the centuries, the castles fared better than the urban walls, most of which disappeared. Towns and cities spread their bounds, and metropolitan land became too sought-after to waste on an old wall (exceptions include the surviving stretches of wall in York, Canterbury, Chester and Colchester, all now great tourist attractions).

The walls may have gone, but in some places they.retain a sort of ghostly imprint. Their one-time presence is recorded in the shape of footpaths that follow the old stone foundations. In Sandwich, Kent, a graceful promenade curves round the central node of this ancient Cinque Port town. Sandwich, situated at the point where the River Stour meets the Channel, was once one of the most prosperous townships in England. As a port, it traded around Europe and beyond. But its trading power spawned many enemies and jealous rivals. It badly needed a thick defensive wall. Times changed, the harbour silted up, trade moved elsewhere. No longer required, the walls were dismantled, or in places just toppled over. But local people continued their habit of walking the boundary line where the walls had once stood, and do so to this day.

Sandwich, Kent. The defensive wall round the old Cinque Port has long gone, but it has left a trace in the shape of the promenade that still encircles part of the town centre.

Anyone who imagines that Sandwich is tops in the vanished glory stakes should visit the village of Pleshey, in Essex. Buried in the countryside and notoriously hard to find in pre-sat-nav days, Pleshey scores high in terms of charm and prettiness. But few places can ever have fallen so far and so fast from eminence to picturesque insignificance. Shortly after the Norman Conquest, Pleshey was established as the administrative and military centre of the shire. Presiding over it was the great Geoffrey de Mandeville, 1st Earl of Essex. Not content with being Warden of the Tower of London, Geoffrey set about constructing a castle stronghold of his own, one that would match his, and Pleshey's, status. The castle, begun around 1135, was designed to be one of the grandest in England, but de Mandeville added an extra mark of distinction. The little township at the base of the castle was enclosed by a low earth rampart (as uncertain in its origin as the Devil's Dyke). De Mandeville upgraded this embankment, presenting Pleshey with its very own town wall. (Town walls weren't just defensive, they were also symbols of wealth and importance. When Charles II wanted to punish the citizens of Coventry for supporting the Parliamentary cause, he ordered the destruction of the city's walls.)

De Mandeville never lived to see the completion of his castle. He chose the losing side in the Anarchy, the civil war that raged between 1138 and 1153, and died an inconspicuous death in a skirmish. The de Mandeville' family fortunes collapsed, and Pleshey Castle soon began to crumble in sympathy. Centuries later, it was identified as a symbol of forlorn neglect by no less a judge than William Shakespeare. In *The Tragedy of Richard II*, the widow of the murdered Thomas, Duke of Gloucester, is confined to the freezing ruin. As well she might, she bewails 'the empty lodgings and unfurnished walls, unpeopled offices, untrodden stones'.

The stones of the castle may have been untrodden, but that clearly could not be said of Pleshey's township wall. Today, the course of the old wall is marked by a ring of trees and also by another testimonial. The fortifications have gone, but once again, the right of way proved less prone to decay. The footpath curves protectively around Pleshey, as if it still has a job to do in proclaiming the village's importance. It has proved more resilient than any great castle or magniloquent title.

Pleshey, Essex. A peaceful village that once had much grander pretensions. The encircling trees mark the line of the old town rampart, as does the accompanying footpath. The castle mound is visible left-centre. (Aerial photo: Edward Clack)

5

Ancient Mysteries

There are ancient presences, from the Pyramids to Stonehenge, that haunt us with an air of impenetrable mystery. Their ultimate riddle can never be fully broached, even by scientific methods. A number of Britain's ancient pathways have a place in this enigmatic catalogue.

One path sub-species exudes a particularly strong aura. They are the 'old straight tracks' that stretch from one ancient artefact – earth mounds, sarsen stones, hilltop cairns, pagan places of worship – to another. Early in the twentieth century, these tracks, with their sense of strange purpose, captivated the imagination of a photographer and amateur historian named Alfred Watkins. So much so that this son of Herefordshire introduced a new word into the English language to describe them – 'leylines'.

In fact, leylines make sense at the most practical of levels. At a time when there were no maps or official signposts, they enabled cross-country travellers to navigate from landmark to landmark, sightline to sightline. The mystery lies in the accuracy of their surveying and the way that hilltop burial mounds are lined up in such (no pun intended) dead-straight rows, as if the final act of the deceased was to guide the living in their journeys across the land.

Arthur's Stone. a Neolithic burial mound high above the Golden Valley, in Herefordshire. It was identified by Alfred Watkins as a landmark and focal point for 'leyline' tracks traversing the Welsh Borders.

Watkins judged the leylines to be pre-Roman. Although no one recorded the birth of the old straight tracks, the process of travel from landmark to landmark had an ancient parallel at sea. The National Maritime Museum at Greenwich houses examples of 'bone maps' that are around 10,000 years old. Indents of various shapes and depths are chipped into the bones to indicate coastal landmarks. Guides like these have been used by mariners tacking along coastlines since time immemorial, and could well have influenced the leyline surveyors. But this is no more provable or otherwise than the notion, much postulated in the 1970s, that the leylines had been 'leyed' down by extraterrestrial beings. The leylines can never be explained dogmatically, allowing the old straight tracks to retain their ancient sense of mystery, as well as their special appeal, simply as ramblers' pathways.

There is no mystery as to the purpose of the Broomway. The mystery lies in the fact that it exists. Any answer is subterranean, inaccessible beneath lethal quicksands.

The Broomway is a 3-mile, ramrod straight trackway across the seabed. It follows the coastline of Foulness Island, at the mouth of the Thames Estuary, about 300 yards offshore. Needless to say, it is accessible only at low tide.

The lonely Broomway track, photographed on a raw January day in 1973, as a lethal sea mist starts to roll in from the Maplin Sands. (Photo: Ron Case)

Not for nothing has it been dubbed the Doomway. On either side of the trackway lie the Blacksands, villainous quicksands that grapple humans or horses, and hold them immovable until the tide moves in and drowns them. Yet, the 30-foot-wide Broomway remains as hard as concrete. Somehow it has defied the pounding and scouring of the surf since time immemorial. Some kind of tough but narrow base supports the Broomway. The nature of this substructure is unknown, since archaeological excavation is impossible on these sucking sands. Whatever that base consists of, it has allowed the Broomway to withstand even the full force of the North Sea, patiently attacking it, century after century, without shifting an inch.

One local historian believes that the answer lies in a natural outcrop of chalk, thrusting up through the estuarine sands and slimy clay. If so, this sliver-thin, ruler-straight aberration is a true gift of the geological gods.

Whatever its origins, the Broomway has been an integral part of life on Foulness since man initially settled there. The first written mention is in the manorial records for 1415, where it is clear that the track through the sea was already regarded as ancient, and near miraculous.

Farmers on the island have taken a practical approach to the semi-miracle. For them it has always been an invaluable line of communication to the mainland. Foulness Island is pierced by numerous tidal creeks, most of which were only finally bridged in the twentieth century. Before this happened, the creeks presented a time-consuming and sometimes dangerous obstacle to anyone trying to enter or leave Foulness. By contrast, the Broomway at low tide was a veritable super highway. It was reliable and speedy, and it required no maintenance. On the downside, it could be relied on to kill you if you failed to get the tide times right, or strayed off the narrow ribbon of track onto the soft sand and mud. An added hazard has always been the sea mist. Emerging in moments as if from nowhere, it can suddenly swirl around the path, blanking out all vision. The gravestones in Foulness churchyard testify to the regular loss of life. It included, on one occasion, the rector of Foulness.

By way of guidance, the locals resorted to a unique device. Into the hard sand they drove upended besoms (witches' broomsticks) at 30-yard intervals, on either side of the pathway. Thus the Broomway got its name. The brooms have gone, but the path through the sea – and the right of way that goes with it – remain, unchanging and implacable as ever, outfacing the sea itself.

6

Paths in the Life of the Land

The footpath network, as explained in the introduction, has a voracious inventory of sources, ranging from Ice Age animal tracks to bypassed twentieth-century trunk roads. By far the commonest, however, is the simple field path, trodden out by country people going about their work, and vital to the life of the land.

Weary harvest workers, pictured alongside the track (on right) that takes them to and from their labours. A graphic depiction of the role that field paths played in the working life of the land. The scene, drawn by Hubert von Herkomer, is from Thomas Hardy's classic novel of English country life *Tess of the d'Urbevilles.*

In the beginning, field paths bloomed along with the advance of agriculture itself, as the human population moved away from hunter-gathering, and as woods and heath gave way to productive fields. These weren't travellers' paths. They were the precise opposite to long-distance routes like the ridgeways or the Peddars Way. They were country paths, not cross-country paths.

The countryside has always abounded in recording angels, but few of these scribes saw fit to mention anything as ordinary as a field path. Here and there, however, their story can be traced on the ground, across the millennia.

As in other respects, the Romans left their signature. They were among the first to develop an organised system of agriculture, based on field systems (although in some cases they may simply have developed existing Celtic-era farmscapes). The orderly Roman enclosures were accessed by an equally well-organised grid system of tracks, some of which survive as footpaths.

A typical series of Roman pathways runs from the north shore of the Thames Estuary for an average of about 4 miles into the hinterland.[1] They bear the most famous hallmark of Roman construction, inasmuch as they are straight. These, however, were not strategic Roman highways like Stane Street or the Fosse Way but access tracks, constructed at regular intervals to service the farms along Thameside. The Romans loved this stretch of their empire. The marshlands along the shoreline are studded with salt workings, which exported this precious material as far afield as Rome itself. Then, a mile or so inland, where

Part of a Roman farm track, which survives in fragments north of the Thames Estuary. Around 1170, this already ancient path was used as a boundary line to define the newly created Essex parishes of Ramsden Crays and Ramsden Bellhouse.

the ground slopes upwards in a series of low gravelly hills, they set up a concentration of villas and farmsteads. This is still one of the driest areas in Britain, and the south-facing, sunny slopes held a clear appeal to the Mediterranean settlers. Excavations at Prittlewell have even found evidence of a Roman vineyard.

In a later era, these farm tracks were used by pilgrims, heading south to Canterbury. Many have been built over. Others survive as country lanes. But a number of stretches survive in their original capacity as farm tracks, with 2,000 years of service to agriculture to their name.

Even the Romans could only make limited inroads into wild Britannia. At the time of their departure in 410, most of the land remained as uncultivated forest and heath. But the march of agriculture continued down the centuries, spearheaded by the monasteries. Agricultural pioneers cut tracks, and advanced along them, carving productive fields out of the wild woods. The process even had a name: 'assarting'. Initially it left a landscape of small fields and thick wooded hedges and numerous surviving small woods. But across most of the countryside the fields steadily enlarged, eventually creating the modern, more wide-open landscape of today. Many assarting tracks have disappeared as a result.

Yet, in a number of places, something of the original assart landscape has been preserved, providing a glimpse of the means by which the land was opened up for agriculture, and the paths that made this possible.

One example lies on the rising uplands to the north of the River Nene in Northamptonshire. Early medieval settlers made a base on the riverbank and set out on a systematic process of assarting, cutting tracks, felling trees and ploughing the ground that they had cleared.[2] The tracks they made remain as footpaths, fanning out from the riverbank. At the top of the ridge, the paths arrive at a small wood that survived the advance of the assarters. Its name: Assart Coppice.

Field paths developed organically. As the countryside opened up for agriculture, the footpath system grew alongside it. Field paths emerged as part of the workaday world of labour and survival. But while times and people changed, the old paths never went away.

The Industrial Revolution of the late eighteenth and early nineteenth century changed the world forever. Until then, around 95 per cent of the population lived in the countryside and worked in agriculture, or its related trades. For the most part, their only means of transport was by foot – their own. Paths were stitched into their existence. Shortcuts across the fields and heaths were more than a just a mere convenience. The importance attached to footpaths in the life of the countryside can be gauged by two major Common Law decisions, laid down by the high courts in the seventeenth century. The case of *James v Hayward (1630)* established that the erection of a gate across a public field path amounted to a nuisance in law. In this instance, the gate hadn't even been locked or fastened. Mere blockage of the path amounted to a civil wrongdoing. Then in *Griesly's Case (1669)*, the great King's Bench justice Sir Peyton Ventis determined that the ploughing of a field path also amounted to a nuisance in law. In both cases, the courts firmly took the side of the pedestrian over the property owner. In doing so, they would have drawn on the ancient Roman *Jus Ambulandi* (see Chapter 4) as a precedent.

For the country people, observed by the poet Thomas Gray, homeward plodding their weary way as evening descended, paths were a fundamental of life. They also acted as a haven, the only available haven, for courting couples, as the numerous lovers'

An assarting path in Northamptonshire passes the abandoned Elizabethan summer residence Lyveden New Bield. Tracks like this were key to developing the uplands of the River Nene valley for agriculture.

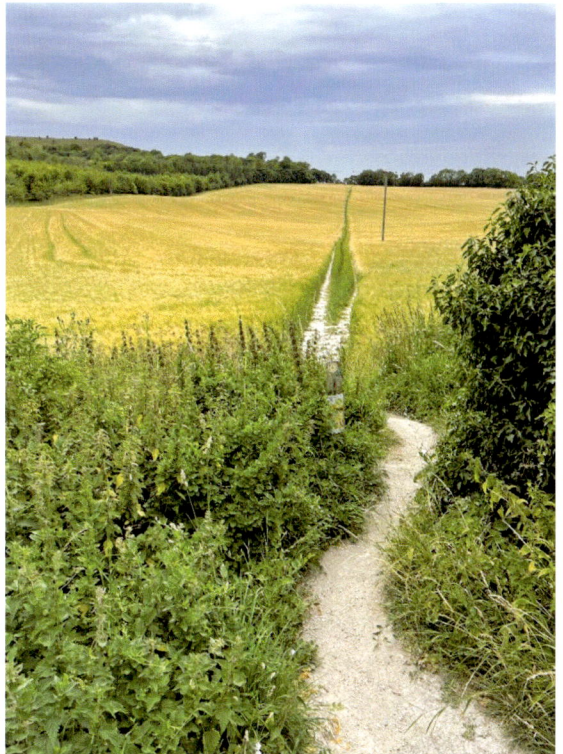

A densely grown modern field crop near Ellacombe, in Buckinghamshire, makes use of every square inch of space. But room still has to be allowed for the old field path that bisects it.

An illustration to the lyrical poem 'Elegy Written in a Country Churchyard', by Thomas Gray, first published in 1751. As night descends, weary field workers take the footpath home, watched from a parish churchyard by the poet. (Artist unidentified)

lanes scattered around the country testify. So there are good reasons why the closure of footpaths has always aroused such ferocious opposition. Country people took their footpaths for granted until they were threatened. Then they mobilised. In protecting their right to walk ancient thoroughfares, the working population deferred to no one and no place. John Skinner was the disputatious rector of Camerton, Somerset.[3] In 1819, he attempted to limit access to an ancient path, the Church Walk, used for generations for the passage of coffins. Skinner's argument was that it was indeed a church walk, since it ran through church property. The villagers promptly formed a walking club, dedicated to use of the Church Walk, day and night, simply to exercise their right to do so. The path stayed open.

The value placed on footpaths has been expressed in solid, monumental form. Maud Heath sold eggs for a living. Several times a week she tramped from her home in the Wiltshire village of Langley Burrell to sell her wares in Chippenham market. The flood plains around the River Avon can be boggy, or worse. Maud's trek often involved wading up to her knees in water. When Maud died in 1474, she bequeathed her estate to fund a dry path for her successors. Maud Heath's Causeway rises on sixty-four arches which carry it across the waterlogged meadows.

Maud, the path benefactor, became venerated as an almost saintly figure in the Wiltshire countryside. A monument to her was erected on Wick Hill above the causeway, and a local vicar wrote a poem in her honour, which includes the lines: 'Maud Heath's Pathway winds in shade and light/Christian wayfarer in a world of strife/Be still and consider the Path of Life.'

Maud Heath's Causeway, Wiltshire, a raised footway over the River Avon marshes in Wiltshire. The eponymous Maud spent her life tramping through boggy ground to sell eggs in Chippenham market. When she died, around 1475, she bequeathed her savings to construct a drier route for her successors.

Farmers and landowners, not surprisingly, tended to take a different stance. For them, rural footpaths were often just seen as a nuisance, or worse. We are privy to this hostility as it existed over 400 years ago, thanks to the agriculturist Thomas Tusser (d. 1580). Having farmed at various sites in Essex and Suffolk, Tusser drew on his working experience to write *Five Hundred Points of Good Husbandry*. Published in 1562, this was the first ever manual about agricultural practice in the English language. Immensely popular, it is thought to have outsold any other non-religious book in the Elizabethan era.

Along with advice on every aspect of farming and horticulture, Tusser also uses his pages to rail against a whole range of enemies, ranging from idle and drunken farm labourers to dodgy neighbours. A special level of rage erupts when it comes to the subject of public footpaths across his farm. He regarded these as pestilential corridors, carrying all sorts of undesirables across his crops and through his diligently cultivated cow pastures and orchards. 'What footpathes are made, and how brode [broad], annoiance too much to be borne', the hard-pressed farmer fulminated, preceding similar sentiments expressed by motoring journalist turned farmer Jeremy Clarkson, 450 years later.[4] Yet like so many others, Tusser recognised that he could do nothing against path power. Legal rights of way prevailed. 'The farmer they leave in the lash, with laws on every side,' he concluded.

One reason for Tusser's hatred of footpaths was their use by poachers. As long as a suspected poacher was in motion across a public right of way, he could not be evicted or challenged. Even the owner of the land remained powerless.

In 1824, Yorkshire landowner Charles Waterton found a novel way to outwit poachers. Waterton was a passionate naturalist. He had travelled the world, studied nature in all its

Farm labourers at work in winter, pruning an orchard. This Flemish illustration was used as the frontispiece for Thomas Tusser's *Five Hundred Points of Good Husbandry*. For Tusser, a working Suffolk farmer, tracks like the one visible in the picture were fine for agricultural purposes, but he objected strongly when the public exercised their right to use them.

forms, and witnessed at first hand the destruction of the natural world that was already underway. When he returned to Walton Hall, the ancestral home of the Watertons, he set about transforming the entire property into a nature reserve, the first dedicated conservation zone on record anywhere in the world. But his efforts were plagued by poachers, making free with the old country footpaths through the hall grounds. Waterton didn't try to close the paths. He simply made them obsolete, by throwing open the entire grounds to the public (with the exception of a few carefully preserved and guarded spaces). Amateur naturalists flocked to Walton Hall, day and night. Their eyes and ears proved a far more effective deterrent against poachers than any number of gamekeepers.

The generations who trod out the field paths had narrow horizons. They would never have thought of their local paths as belonging to any sort of wider highway system. Within this limited sphere, the paths did acknowledge two crucial focal points. One was the parish church, the other was the nearest pub. Time and again, the map depicts these two institutions lying at the hub of a right-of-way network, like local traffic-control centres. Paths radiate from the graveyard and the pub garden (now usually the pub car park) like spokes from a wheel.

One of the remoter pubs in south-east England is the Royal Oak, nearest settlement Chilgrove, in West Sussex. The old shepherds' hostelry lies in a wooded hollow, 2 miles

Village church and village pub, close neighbours all over Britain. Country footpaths homed in on these two rural institutions. (John Chater)

from the nearest road of any size. But what it lacks in roads, the pub makes up for in paths. No less than seven ancient trackways converge on the Oak. They lead in different directions out onto the lonely South Downs. The old hill men lived an isolated existence, seeing only their sheep and dogs for days on end. Unlike other members of the farming community, they didn't have the promise of regular market days, where they could meet and drink with their own kind. But the tracks that led to the Royal Oak would have promised conviviality when it was needed, and the company of fellow spirits, when the sheep permitted.

Another country watering hole that speaks to the partnership of pubs and footpaths is the Hook and Glove, in the village of Farley, near Salisbury. A footpath leads to the front door. A footpath leads to the back door. And a right of way through the bar room connects the two, although few users show the willpower to ignore the bar and make an uninterrupted journey.

As for churches, their gravitational pull was at least equal to that of the local watering hole. Churches acted not just as centres of worship and gateways to the hereafter, but as hubs of local and international news and gossip, underpinners of social order, and political as well as spiritual pulpits. Their towers and spires dominated local landscapes across the British Isles. Churchyards may have been places of the dead, but all local life converged there, and that included footpaths. (As the poet Sir John Betjeman pointed out in a BBC radio broadcast: 'You can generally assume that a country church is old if the map shows dotted lines of footpaths leading to it.'[5])

Like numerous other pubs, the Ramblers' Rest at Chiselhurst, Kent, has been a focal point for generations of footpath users – and has the name to prove it.

The parish church as footpath hub. St Andrew's Church, Wood Walton, stands isolated and remote in thinly populated farmland north of Huntingdon. Six separate footpaths converge on the church from different directions, a testimony to its importance in the lives of isolated workers on the land.

Stiles, set into the wall or hedge, are almost as regular a feature in churchyards as gravestones. They testify to the weekly footpath journeys of parish and farm folk to the places where their ancestors lay. Along the way, the paths also played another intermediary role in the life cycle. Their role as lovers' lanes, the natural resort for trysts, flirtations and courtships, gave a streak of romance too many an otherwise unassuming field track. Victorian artists picked up on this association.

One other basic factor has also been at play. This is the British passion for walking as a leisure and social pursuit. Richard Burchett's painting *Corn Field in the Isle of Wight* captures the way that country paths exercised their highway right, pushing their way through the fields ruthlessly, with no concern for standing crops.

The young woman in the painting demonstrates something else. With the arrival of railways, the migration of the population to industrial cities and mass ownership of bicycles, the crucial importance of field paths to the country economy began to wane. At the same time, however, they were acquiring a new identity, as sources of delight.

A stone slab designed to carry footpath users over the churchyard wall of the Norman church in Fobbing, Essex. The path passes in a direct line to a corresponding slab, set in the far side of the enclosing wall.

HE LOVES ME - HE LOVES ME NOT.

Young lovers also had their uses for footpaths, as celebrated in this light-hearted postcard. One of a series based on country life in Devon, published around 1900. (Raphael Tuck archive)

An ambling country footpath winds its way through fields, hedges and coverts on the Isle of Wight. A young woman enjoys a leisurely stroll, taking advantage of a path that would have been used by agricultural workers for centuries. A detail from a mid-nineteenth-century painting by Richard Burchett.

7

Boundaries

Many field paths and cart tracks acquired an additional and rather grander role, as boundary lines. Ancient ways were convenient. They lent themselves naturally to the business of dividing up the nation. They were tangible and long established. They precluded future border rows and land grabs, in cases where boundary lines were more vague. Nobody could argue about the exact position of an ancient track.

A path that acts as an administrative border must, by definition, be venerable. The founding father of landscape history, W. G. Hoskins, stated a basic principle. When roads or tracks are followed continuously 'by parish boundaries [it is] always a sign of great antiquity in a road'.[1] What applied to parishes applies equally to other administrative borders, including county boundaries and, in one case, a national border.

The modern local-government structure, based on counties and parishes, has its roots in Anglo-Saxon England.[2] It continued apace, almost without a blip, after the Norman Conquest. Many an anonymous footpath found itself basking in sudden bureaucratic significance. The most spectacular case, all 177 miles of it, is Offa's Dyke. The earthwork, topped by a long-distance footpath, still provides the boundary between England and Wales for a not inconsiderable part of its length. It seldom departs more than a short distance from the modern border.

One step down from this international role are the ancient tracks that act as county, or shire, borders. For instance, the pre-Roman Sewstern Lane provided a quick and easy means to define the boundary between Leicestershire and Lincolnshire. At around the same time, Saxon political fixers picked on a track known as the Shire Rack to decide the border between Dorset and Wiltshire. The Shire Rack had venerable credentials. It ran (and still runs) through Cranborne Chase, described by Thomas Hardy as 'the oldest wood in England'.[3]

Hundreds, perhaps thousands, of miles of ancient footpath help to define parish borders. Just one example will suffice. While not quite in the Offa's Dyke's league, another earthwork and footpath that does sterling work as a boundary is Grim's Dyke (also known as the Mongewell Ditch), in the Oxfordshire/Buckinghamshire Chilterns. The Anglo-Saxon land commissioners clearly regarded it as a godsend. They used a 3½-mile stretch of Grim's Dyke to define the boundaries of four separate parishes: Crowmarsh, Ipsden, Nuffield

The Offa's Dyke footpath, south-east of Montgomery, Powys. At this point, Offa's Dyke acts as the modern-day boundary between England, to the right of the embankment, and Wales, to the left.

The ancient cattle road known as Sewstern Lane acts as a boundary line between Leicestershire and Lincolnshire. (Painting by David Gentleman, courtesy of the Shell Archive)

Grim's Dyke, a straight embankment of unknown origin, runs 4 miles east from the River Thames, in Oxfordshire. It was used to establish the border of four medieval parishes.

and Benson.[4] But they had no better idea than anyone else as to its origins. Even then, it belonged to the misty past. Their land charter from 950 refers to Grim's Dyke as 'than Ealden Wagen' – 'the old way'.

The steady process of dividing Britain into counties and parishes was accompanied by a parallel development. The same sense of tidy organisation applied. But if anything the process was conducted even more determinedly. This was enclosure. Steadily, remorselessly, the one-time forest land, and the open spaces, were divided into hedged fields. Hedge-laying (a skill that rapidly developed into a stand-alone rural craft and commercial activity) didn't stop when it came to an established footpath. The hedge-layers simply laid their hawthorn and blackthorn across the path. But the rights of way remained, as did the need of agricultural workers to gain access to all those neat new 10-acre fields that had been created by the hedgerow grids. By way of a solution, there emerged a device that came to symbolise British footpaths: the stile.

The most common and familiar type of stile is the crossover post-and-plank, but a variety of other types emerged, many of them quite picturesque. The stile, a simple utilitarian device, somehow acquired a poetic and even moral resonance. In the nursery rhyme 'There was a Crooked Man', a stile plays a starring role. The crooked man finds a crooked sixpence

A typical enclosure landscape of 10-acre fields divided by hedges. An ancient field path exerts its ancient right, piercing the hedge and allowing harvesters to move from field to field. The scene, drawn in 1838 by William Henry Prior, depicts Tufnell Park in North London, with the Great North Road in the distance. The entire area has since been developed for housing and the Holloway women's prison building.

'against a crooked stile'. In mid-Victorian England, a strange trend developed for daubing literary and biblical quotations on stiles. In Shakespeare's *The Winter's Tale*, the vagabond rogue Autolycus exhorts us to embrace the roaming life, in lines that provide the epigraph for this book:

> Jog on, jog on, the footpath way
> And merrily hent [grab] the stile-a.
> Your merry heart goes all the way
> Your sad tires in a mile-a.[5]

A ladder stile, near Pendle Hill, Lancashire.

An aptly named 'squeezer' stile, in the Weald.
(Illustration by T. Mansell, from *The Wayfarer's
Book*, 1952)

SPEAK EVIL OF NO MAN

A religious admonition on a stile near Stinsford, Dorset. Messages like this were inscribed by itinerant preachers who roamed the countryside. (Drawing, 1906, by Edmund New)

8

Path Wars

In March 1902, the legendary educationalist Dorothea Beale, headmistress of Cheltenham Ladies' College, founder of St Hilda's College, Oxford, doughty champion of women's education and equally doughty champion of suffragettism, rattled off a stern letter to the local authority. Stern letters were something she had been rattling off all her life, but this one was different. It concerned a footpath.[1]

Young ladies at Britain's most renowned establishment for young females had been used to taking the path up Leckhampton Hill – a giant Cotswold presence that looms over the town of Cheltenham. There they botanised, or painted watercolours, or simply absorbed the spiritual values of the great view over the Severn Valley to the Welsh hills. Leckhampton Hill was, for them, a vital outdoor classroom.

The path up Leckhampton Hill, Gloucestershire, battleground for one of the great footpath controversies.

However, now, suddenly, it was closed off, and the formidable Miss Beale was having none of it.

Miss Beale had written a history of Britain, largely centred on great battles such as Hastings and Waterloo. Did she realise, though, that she was now a participant in an ongoing battle that had flared up in different parts of the country, down the centuries? The battle of the footpaths.

Either way, the closure of the Leckhampton path was soon being described, locally, in terms of a military engagement. Indeed, an epic poem published in 1904 by one George Townsend was entitled 'The Battle of Leckhampton Hill'.

Hostilities were precipitated by businessman Henry Dale. Dale acquired ownership of Leckhampton from its previous owners, who had adopted a benevolent attitude to public access. The new owner was in a different mould. He wanted to monetise the hill. His schemes involved building residential villas across much of the rural estate, and expanding the existing limestone quarry operation, both at the expense of public access. All this on a beloved hillside that was moulded into the heart of Cheltenham. It wasn't just the young ladies of the college who benefitted from the open air and views. Access to Leckhampton had been enjoyed by the town's population since time immemorial. Now suddenly that access was blocked off.

Dale's approach was confrontational. He placed barriers across some of the footpaths, and challenged the council to remove them. On another spot, he built a cottage for the quarry foreman. The cottage was positioned, provocatively, to block the main right of way up the hill.

It didn't take long before the whole of Cheltenham was up in arms. On 15 July 1902, a large crowd congregated in the town centre. It grew in size, according to a reporter, 'like a rolling snowball'. Around 2,000 townsfolk then marched up Leckhampton. They chased the occupants out of the cottage, then dragged out the furniture and burnt it. After that, the cottage 'was razed to the ground, without a stone left standing'. Police were present in force, 'but powerless to act where such a large and determined mob were concerned'.

Defiantly, Mr Dale rebuilt the cottage in exactly the same position. Again, a huge crowd marched up the hill. Standing on a wagon that had been drawn up outside the cottage, Charles Barrett, a local gardener, addressed the crowd. He was one of an organised group of protesters who had dubbed themselves the Leckhampton Stalwarts. 'Men of Leckhampton', he cried. 'Our footpath is railed off. We are here today to assert our rights.' The cottage was then smashed up (though less comprehensively this time).

Eight of the ringleaders were jailed, and there was no further destruction or threat of violent public protest. The battleground switched to the law courts, and eventually to the Court of Chancery in London.

But Henry Dale seems to have been worn down by the prolonged battle, as well as the legal expenses. He never surrendered formally, but the court's conclusion seemed indecisive, and the Battle of Leckhampton Hill simply fizzled out. The footpaths remained open. Dale sold up, and the Leckhampton estate was eventually acquired by the local authority as a public open space, in perpetuity. It was opened by the Mayor of Cheltenham in September 1929. But a faint aroma of conflict continued to hang about the hill, and as late as the 1960s there were still old men in Cheltenham who talked proudly about their role in the battle of the Leckhampton footpaths.

The narrative of Leckhampton Hill is a reminder that, anciently established though they may be, the long-term survival of footpaths can never be taken for granted. But the response to closure has seldom been supine. As a passionate dispute between landowner and footpath users, Leckhampton is typical of many similar cases. Only the scale of the dispute, galvanising an entire town, and escalating into riots, sets it somewhat apart. Britons will defend their footpaths with a ferocity unknown in other places. Nick Levinson, a retired BBC producer, recalls trying to organise a protest against the wholesale closure of tracks in the Italian village where he now lives. 'Everyone just shrugged their shoulders,' he says. 'The attitude is, "we don't want to cause any trouble".'

On at least one occasion, footpath passion erupted into full-scale murder, and lethal justice. It has been said that the French commit murder for love, the Italians for power, the Americans for money and the Spanish for wounded pride. But only the British would commit murder over the issue of a right to walk.

On 17 March 1830, a fisherman (and champion Thames boatsman), William Malcolm, landed on the sea wall at Shellhaven Creek, off the southern side of the Thames Estuary. He sold some fish to a cottager, Mrs Elizabeth Baker, then headed back to his boat. As he crossed a meadow footpath, he was spotted by the local landowner, Captain Moir. The pair had already quarrelled over fishing rights. Moir pursued Malcolm on horseback,

Knole, a fifteenth-century stately home in Sevenoaks, Kent. In June 1884 the then owner, Lord Sackville, closed off a path through Knole Park. The route had been enjoyed, unchallenged, by local people since time immemorial. What resulted were, in the chief constable's words, 'riotous and tumultuous proceedings'. A crowd of 1,500 townspeople tore down the barriers erected by Sackville and used them to block his lordship's front door. Knole is now the property of the National Trust, and the public retains full use of the path.

A right of way dispute that turned bloody. The 1830 murder of fisherman William Malcolm by landowner Captain Moir depicted in an illustration for a contemporary 'penny dreadful'.

and challenged the fisherman as a trespasser. Malcolm maintained that he was simply exercising an ancient right to walk along the footpath through the meadow. The exchange became more heated. Then a shot rang out.

Malcolm died days later as a result of complications from the bullet wound. Witnesses' evidence was enough to convict Moir of wilful murder. Following his trial at Chelmsford assizes, he was hanged in public beside the bridge over the River Chelmer.

The case became a considerable cause célèbre. The result was hailed as symbolic. It signalled that nobody could get away with murder, however rich and powerful the protagonist, however humble the victim. A ballad published immediately after Moir's execution hailed the justice of the sentence, as well as the right of any Briton to exercise a fundamental liberty, the right to walk unchallenged along a public footpath:

> O never let the rich and proud
> Oppress the humble poor:
> For God for such hard-heartedness
> Has still a vengeance sure ..
> Poor William Malcolm's sole offence
> Was walking on his ground
> At which the haughty captain soon
> A grudge towards him found.

Yet, there was nothing inevitable about the development and survival of the footpath system. Ireland, which has a widely similar landscape of small fields, hedge and spinneys, has its fair share of ancient trackways and field paths, but not the wide-ranging right of public access to go with them. The passionate upholding of the right to walk seems to be a phenomenon limited to the British mainland. Nick Levinson contrasts British footpath fever with the attitude in his local Tuscan village. 'Landowners have fenced off and blocked most of the ancient trackways,' he says. 'When I tried to organise a response, the attitude everywhere was, no, let it be, it's not worth putting ourselves out.'

The championing of footpaths has passed, in a steady process, from ad hoc campaigners to local authorities. Corporations learnt how to wheel out the heavy guns and also how to organise publicity to their favour. In 1908, Marsden Council, in West Yorkshire, went to court to defend the right of walkers to use the old packhorse route across Clowes Moor. The lord of the manor had sought to bar access. A motley group of witnesses, including shepherds and drovers, was assembled to testify in favour of the unchallenged right of way. They were photographed at Marsden station on the morning of the court battle, all set for next day's front pages across the North of England.

Another star witness, at the other end of the twentieth century, was John Evans.[2] In October 1989, the former coalminer appeared at an inquiry to prove a right of way on a footpath between Fforest-fach and Gowerton, West Glamorgan. Mr Evans was 112 at the time, and authenticated as the oldest man ever to live in the UK. He well remembered walking the path, unchallenged, as a boy. Naturally, his evidence clinched the issue.

Even the German Luftwaffe, Britain's enemy in the Second World War, has managed to contribute to feuds of a different nature, this time concerning footpaths. Between 1939 and 1940, German reconnaissance aircraft systematically photographed every square mile of southern and eastern England, in preparation for an invasion. The portfolio was seized by American forces at the end of the war. Years later, the photographs from these reconnaissance missions were consulted in disputes at Malton, North Yorkshire (1995), and Shipton Gorge, Dorset (1996). In both cases, the images proved crucial. They established the presence of certain pre-war footpaths, despite claims that they had never existed.

Countless foot soldiers have thrown themselves into the ongoing battle to preserve our footpaths. But if footpaths have a consecrated hero, even a national patron saint, it has to be a modest craftsman from the early eighteenth century named Timothy Bennett. The story of the cobbler of Bushy Park illustrates both the passion aroused by footpaths, and how path power can outweigh even the mightiest and wealthiest individuals.

The 2nd Lord Halifax was known as one of the grandest, haughtiest noblemen in the land. Among his titles was that of Ranger of Bushy Park. In 1734 he chose to eradicate, peremptorily, the ancient footpath running through the park from Hampton Wick to Hampton Court.

Witnesses gathered at Marsden station on 30 March 1908, on the morning of the packhorse-trail court hearing at Leeds Assizes. Thanks to their testimony, the trail remains open as a public right of way. (Marsden History Group)

Timothy Bennett, who owned a cobbler's shop at Hampton Wick, took exception to the closure. In his own punning words, he 'pledged his awl' (the sum total of his wealth) to fight the case in court. But first he gained an audience with Lord Halifax to plead the cause personally.

'Begone!' roared Lord Halifax. 'Thou art an impertinent fellow.' But his lordship then took legal advice, and was warned that he would probably lose the case. Unwilling to be humiliated in court by 'a mere cobbling man', Halifax reopened the footpath. Timothy had 'saved the way'.

A memorial to Timothy Bennett was set up in 1900, alongside the eastern entrance to the path he saved. The memorial is really to all those who have fought to preserve rights of way down the centuries. As for TB, his true memorial is the delightful footpath which still curves through the centre of the park. Its name? Cobbler's Walk.

Local authority 'definitive maps' now depict, pretty much once and for all, where footpath rights of way do and do not exist. As a result, the age of contentious closures and

Above left: The memorial to footpath campaigner Timothy Bennett, at the Hampton Wick entrance to Bushy Park, London.

Above right: Cobbler's Walk, the path through Bushy Park, saved for the public by shoemaker Timothy Bennett, and now named in his honour.

fierce legal challenges has passed. It ended, however, with a final flourish. This was thanks to a case that attracted huge national and even international attention, largely because of its central figure. Here was a man who revelled in his self-adopted role as a landowner who took arrogance to the edge of wickedness.

Nicholas van Hoogstraten (an assumed name that translated as 'Van High Streets') was a property dealer of immense wealth and unprincipled methods, which included paying a gang to throw a grenade into the home of a business associate. In 1968 he was sentenced to four years in prison. Lord Justice Wynn said of Hoogstraten that he was 'a sort of self-imagined devil who likes to think of himself as an emissary of Beelzebub.'[3]

Around 1985 Hoogstraten began work on a spectacular building project in the East Sussex countryside. Hamilton Palace, at High Cross, was bigger than Buckingham Palace. The £40 million edifice, complete with giant golden dome, was planned to be his mausoleum. The scheme certainly gained him the enduring attention he craved, but not perhaps in the way he originally conceived.

In 1990 van Hoogstraten blocked off a path across his property, using razor wire, concrete blocks and a pile of (much-photographed) old refrigeration units. A legal battle began, led by the Ramblers Association and East Sussex County Council. Van H wasted no time in describing his highly respectable opponents as 'a bunch of disfranchised perverts'. Ramblers in general he dismissed as 'riff riff' and 'a branch of the dirty mac brigade'. He told a reporter: 'They're disgusting creatures ... I'm not going to open up the footpath. Would you have a lot of Herberts in your garden?' The word got about that he had

THE TIMES SATURDAY JANUARY 15 2000

News 3

'Riff-raff' victorious in battle of the footpath

Nicholas Van Hoogstraten, the property tycoon, is likely to see members of the Ramblers' Association, who he calls riff-raff, walking across his land in the future

Rights of way controversies continued to make headlines until the end of the twentieth century, but after the legal defeat of the 'self-imagined ... emissary of Beelzebub' Nicholas van Hoogstraten, the centuries-old footpath wars effectively came to an end. Here, van Hoogstraten poses in front of the half-finished Hamilton Palace for a newspaper.

threatened to shoot any rambler bold enough to use the footpath. Given his track record, the rumour was taken seriously by some.

By 2003 van H was back in jail, now serving a ten-year sentence for manslaughter, though of a business contact, not a rambler. In February that year, a group of forty walkers removed a padlock from a gate and walked the route that van H had kept closed for thirteen years.

Three decades after the controversy, Hamilton Palace remains a secretive place, hidden behind serried rows of fences and hedges, which have been allowed to grow high and untrimmed. Now only the tip of the palace's golden dome is visible from the footpath. Fierce notices, with the word 'SHOOTING' heavily emphasised, line the pathway. Van H got his wish. Framfield Path No. 9 retains a sense of the indefinably sinister. There is an air of vast and, if pushed, dangerous corporate power, backed by titanic wealth, rocked up on this site. But the aggravating pathway remains open, signposted and regularly used by walkers. NVH made the same discovery as the Earl of Halifax in the eighteenth century, and the powerful quarry owners of Cheltenham in the nineteenth century. Even vast wealth, influence and force of will aren't guaranteed to defeat path power.

The path through the grounds of Hamilton Palace, home of Nicholas van Hoogstraten. The setting for the vicious and much-publicised footpath dispute in 1985, the path is still bordered by fierce keep-out notices.

9

From Highway to Byway

Until the advent of the canal system in the late eighteenth century, packhorses acted as the nation's inland freight carriers. These broad-backed, stout-legged grafters were mostly bred from the Galloway bloodline. They carried the heaviest of goods through some of the most hostile terrain in the British Isles. They could penetrate to places inaccessible by carts, carriages or anything else on wheels, and unlike mules they never whinged about their work. Far from being properly appreciated for their services, they were referenced by the slang term 'Galloway nags'. The phrase, meaning a prostitute, appears in Shakespeare's *The Second Part of King Henry IV*.

The importance of the packhorse supply routes resulted in a level of investment unmatched elsewhere, at a time when even the most important roads were little more than muddy tracks. Packhorse roads were surfaced with a level of technical sophistication not seen in Britain since Roman times. Numerous bridges were especially constructed for the routes. The gift of a packhorse bridge spelt honour and even immortality for a wealthy citizen.

The canals, followed a generation later by the railways, made packhorse transport redundant. But many miles of packhorse roads, along with dozens of packhorse bridges, large and small, remain across the land, as a solid legacy. The bridges are marked by their thinness. Designed for single-file lines of horses, they remain too narrow for four-wheeled vehicles. But they serve ramblers well. One packhorse bridge in particular remains unchallenged as the grandest and most elegant of its kind. This is the Essex Bridge, near Great Haywood, in Staffordshire. Its fourteen arches carry the packhorse road from Cannock Chase, at the point where it crosses the River Trent. The bridge is a showpiece if ever there was one. It was commissioned and paid for in 1570 by the ambitious Walter Deveraux, 1st Earl of Essex, whose residence was at nearby Chartley Castle. Named the Essex Bridge from the word go, it flagged up the earl's munificence, and his concern to boost local commerce.

Along with the bridges, some of the old packhorse road surfaces have slipped comfortably into a new role as leisure footpaths. Their survival is a tribute to their immaculate construction. They have often proved more durable than more modern surfaces of gravel and clinker, particularly on challenging terrain such as moorland.

Galloway horses on a packhorse road approaching Leeds. A print from *Walker's Costumes of Yorkshire*, 1814. (New York Public Library)

The modern highways system eventually reached most corners of Britain, but not all. This illustration shows Bloxworth Heath, Dorset, in the 1890s. Still roadless, the heath is little changed today. Ancient turf paths and tracks continue to provide the only means of access. (Walter Tyndale)

The Long Causeway, a surviving section of seventeenth-century packhorse road, crosses the South Yorkshire moors between Sheffield and Hathersage.

A simple packhorse bridge, one of dozens that survive across Britain. This example is in Slad, Gloucestershire. The old road carried wool from the farms of the high Cotswolds for processing in the mills of the Stroud valleys.

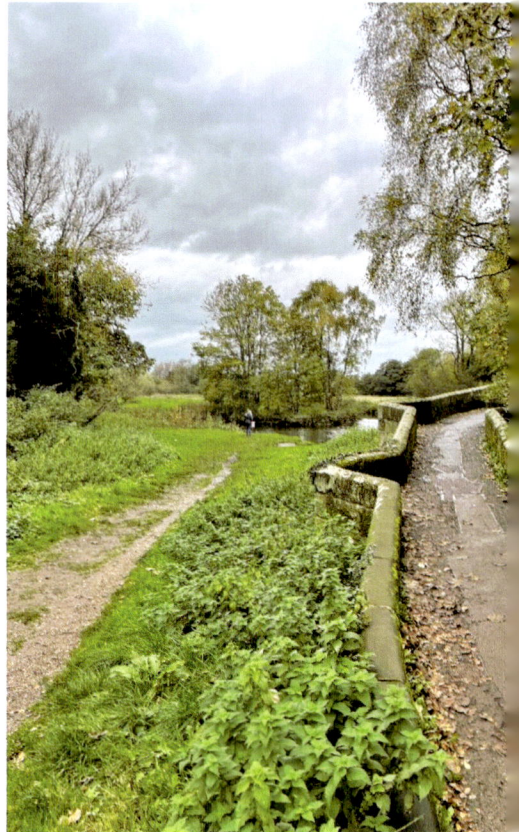

Above left: The Essex Bridge, over the River Trent, at Great Haywood, Staffordshire. It is the longest and most ostentatious packhorse bridge in Britain.

Above right: The Essex Bridge, at the point where it makes landfall in Shugborough Park. For all its splendour, its narrowness means that it is only capable of acting as a footway.

Suddenly, with extraordinary swiftness, Britain became a land of super highways. A new energy was unleashed, spurring construction of thousands of miles of roads, and transforming the speed and reliability of travel. The landmark year was 1663, when the first turnpike trust constructed the first length of turnpike road.[1] The stretch of road, at Wadesmill, in Hertfordshire, still carries traffic along the old A10. It replaced an overused Roman road that had become 'dangerous & ympasable to the great hurt of Travelers and passengers'. (This rogue stretch has now devolved into a pleasant footpath, passing the site of the country's first balloon landing.)

The Wadesmill turnpike was an immediate success, both logistically and commercially. The handsome return it gave to investors helped lead to an explosion of turnpike trusts, and a system of highways that, in speed of delivery and quality of engineering, exceeded anything the Romans had achieved. Just twelve years after the launch of the Wadesmill turnpike, John Ogilby found a ready market when he published the first road atlas.

As the turnpike roads (23,000 miles of them eventually) spread across the land, older, less efficient cross-country roads sank into neglect. They dwindled, as so many Roman roads had done, into quiet, unmanaged green lanes, no longer suitable for wheels but perfect for those travelling on foot.

A fine case study of turnpike development and its impact can be found on the Chiltern escarpment, where the hills descend (some observers have used the term 'plummet') dramatically down to the Midland plain, taking the London–Oxford road with them. The medieval Oxford road at this point presented a notorious challenge, especially in icy weather. Even monarchs, including the magnificent Queen Elizabeth herself, had to resort to walking. Once passengers had demounted, carriages were manoeuvred delicately down the 1:3 descent.

This fearsome route was replaced by a turnpike road in 1719. Instead of diving straight down the hillside, the turnpike engineers constructed a series of loops and hairpins, still followed by traffic on the old A40 today.

But the turnpike in its turn received the bypass treatment. The opening of the M40 motorway consigned the A40 to backroad status, yet another has-been highway.

Those who still elect to drive along it pass the entrance to a bridleway, diverting off to the north-west. This is the medieval road, now a serene trail through the Chiltern beechwood. A short way after the entrance, the trail passes through a wide hollow, cut into the hillside. This was the assembly point, prior to the precipitate descent down the escarpment. Just

The old London–Oxford road, now a footpath, at the point where it begins its precipitate descent down the Chiltern escarpment. It was replaced by an eighteenth-century turnpike road, which achieved the drop via more manageable hairpin bends.

beyond, the footpath commences its steep drop to the Oxfordshire fields below. Even today, the abruptness of the descent is startling. Use of the term plunge is indeed no exaggeration. The turnpikes aroused stiff opposition and even riots in their time. But here, at least, the turnpike must have arrived as a lifesaver and a godsend.

Turnpike trusts (some 1,100 of them by the end of the turnpike era) were entirely private enterprise operations. The 'Revenue Men's Trail', by contrast, was a government scheme. The trail broke new ground in two ways. It was paid for by the first income tax ever levied in the UK, and it was the largest item of government-funded infrastructure ever completed in the country up to that date.

Its purpose was clear-cut: it was built to combat smuggling. Throughout the eighteenth century, smuggling amounted to a massive industry, an endemic crime that dominated the life of maritime communities. Daniel Defoe referred to smuggling as 'the reigning commerce of the English coast'. At one stage it was calculated that one-fifth of all government revenue was lost to this highly organised activity.

The first determined effort to curb the smugglers was made by William Pitt the Younger when he became prime minister in 1783. His premiership coincided with the start of the Napoleonic Wars, which initially gave a boost to the smuggling industry. It was the Pitt government that oversaw construction of a coastal bridleway, stretching for more than 600 miles along the east, south and south-west coasts. The official reason was to act as part of the defences against the anticipated French invasion. But the coast-hugging trail also served to allow swift movement by the customs officers, or 'Revenue Men'. Coastguard stations were set up at regular intervals along the trail, together with coastguard cottages for personnel and their families. Patrols operated along the trail between stations. These operations perhaps contributed more than any other single factor to the decline of smuggling, which had all but vanished from the coast by the mid-nineteenth century.

The coastguard trail was formally incorporated as part of the King's Highway in 1822. Its use by all and sundry meant that, for much of its length, it was already a right of way. Both traditional smugglers and revenue men have vanished from the scene, but their legacy is the coastguard trail, which continues to provide a facility for walkers. It provided a ready-laid basis for the South West Coast Path, Britain's longest designated national trail, completed in 1978.

The Revenue Men's Trail, near Prawle Point, Devon. Here, as elsewhere, it has been adopted to form part of the South West Coast Path.

Smugglers are attacked in their lair by highly mobile officers of the law. Construction of the coastguard path tipped the balance in the Revenue Men's favour. (Unknown artist)

While turnpike highways were being laid down at speed across Britain, a more upmarket type of road was also appearing to serve plusher private estates. This was the private carriage road, much featured in Jane Austen novels. Like the turnpikes, they exploited the new macadamised system for road surfaces to provide a smooth ride, safe from the perils of mud and ruts.

These driveways were often designed for tours of an owner's prized landscape gardens. They also served for shooting parties, and for communication between various parts of sprawling estates.

Like all road surfaces, the carriage roads were expensive to maintain, and many were abandoned when their owners fell on hard times, or lost their estate staff to the trenches of the First World War. Once again the footpath system was the beneficiary.

Some good examples of one-time carriage roads can be walked on the Eridge Park estate, near Tunbridge Wells. They are said to have been built by the Earl of Abergavenny to convey his most honoured house guest, the portly King Edward VII, around the estate. In Cornwall, a carriage road laid down by the Copeland family has been acquired by the National Trust, and forms a scenic promenade alongside the Fal Estuary.

When it comes to lost aristocratic causes, few sites can trump the footpath that runs on a north–south axis through Sherwood Forest, from Welbeck Park to Edwinstowe. At its southern end, almost lost in the trees, is a Gothic archway, dating from 1842. It is inset with statues of Robin Hood, Maid Marian and Friar Tuck (rather slimmed down to fit his niche).

This archway, along with the footpath, is all that transpired of a grand design for a monumental carriage driveway through Sherwood Forest. The Duke of Portland planned a route spanned by twenty such imposing arches. Along the way, the drive would pass within a few feet of the Centre Oak, a giant tree supposedly standing at the dead centre of the forest. The duke was inspired by the Mall in London, beginning as it does with Admiralty

Arch and ending with Buckingham Palace. But the duke's mall through Sherwood Forest would outshine its muse. It would be both longer and archier than London's royal processional route.

The duke had the money and the will to complete his scheme, but he didn't have the time. He died shortly after completion of the first grand archway, and the great Sherwood Forest mall scheme died with him. The wide passageway that was cleared though the forest is still visible, though it is fast being reclaimed by forest vegetation. But in one way, the duke's scheme to open up the forest has been achieved. The grand driveway may never have become a reality, but walkers can follow the entire course of the dream scheme. At least it produced a valuable new footpath.

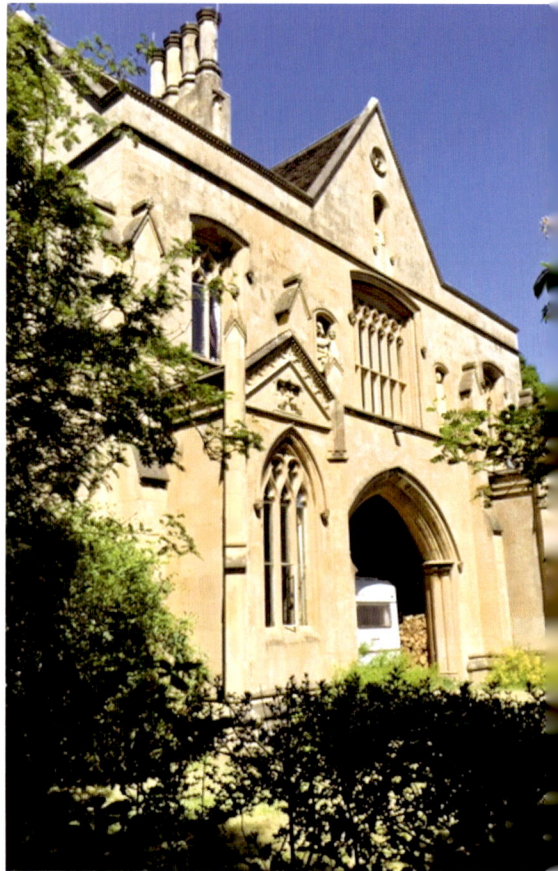

Above left: This footpath is all that remains of the Duke's Drive, planned as a grand procession route through Sherwood Forest.

Above right: The grand arched entrance to the Duke's Drive, now lost and forgotten in the woods.

10

Footprints of Industry

The great industrial works – mines, ironworks, quarries, mills, munitions factories – dominated entire regions, and teemed with human activity. Their chimneys, belching fire, lowered over the landscape. Spoil heaps built up into entire new landscapes. These titans must have seemed imperishable. But then, they were gone, leaving just ruins and a new sort of wilderness. But they did leave footprints.

Often these industries were located in remote areas, such as moors and peak uplands. Networks of tracks built up to service them. The list includes salt ways across the West Midlands, tin miners' tracks in Cornwall, copper miners' tracks on Dartmoor, millstone hewers' tracks in the western Pennines, slate quarrymen's tracks festooning the Welsh valleys and mountains, lead miners' tracks on the moors of Yorkshire and Derbyshire, zinc mines in the Lake District. In some cases, new routes were blazed to serve industries as they developed, elsewhere existing tracks would have found a new purpose as miners' routes. Nowadays it can be hard to disentangle one from the other. Either way, the tracks of vanished industries add up to a hefty tranche of the footpath system.

The Salt Way at the point where it enters the Forest of Arden, Warwickshire. The Salt Way performed a vital role in maintaining the Roman legions in Britain. Salt from the mines in Droitwich was transported east along this route to all areas under Roman occupation.

Mow Cop, Cheshire, on the western edge of the Pennines. An industry making querns (millstones) developed in this area around 1500 BC. The finished products were exported via tracks like this one. The apparent castle is an eighteenth-century folly. (Raphael Tuck archive)

A traditional ore wagon, abandoned alongside the miners' path leading to the old lead workings at Gunnerside, North Yorkshire.

Industrial pathways are at their most appealing in the Weald of Kent and Sussex. They possess a visual appeal that is contrary to everything normally associated with heavy industry. The modern Weald comprises dozens of small woods, laced together by thick, tall hedges. It is an enticing landscape, but that wasn't always the case. Until the early sixteenth century, the Weald was a no-go area, an almost impenetrable forest known by its old name, Andred. The Romans drove a road, Stane Street, through it, from London to the coast, and everyone made sure they kept to the road. Within the forest hungry wolves and murderous brigands prowled.

A one-time iron-industry track, near Burwash Weald, East Sussex. The woods on either side of the track are festooned with old workings from the days when the Weald furnished cannon, shackles, firebacks and railings to the rest of England.

All this changed with the invention of guns and gunpowder. The Weald rapidly developed into Britain's first great industrial heartland.[1] The old forest offered a perfect combination of iron ore, firewood and water, all in abundance. Soon, iron products including cannon, capstans, horseshoes, railings and firebacks were pouring out of the dozens of ironworks that sprang up across the Weald. Once wrought, all these products had to be shipped out of the woods, so the iron masters became as skilled at laying tracks as they were at forging metal.

Metal working migrated to the Midlands in the nineteenth century, the forges closed, and rural peace returned to the Weald. But the ironmasters bequeathed two legacies to this landscape. The dark, still hammer ponds and sluices make up one legacy. The tracks provide the other. They indicate the work of skilled surveyors, not just feet trampling the undergrowth. On these tracks, the grass and weeds grow thinly because they rest on a bed of firm slag, a solid foundation of once red-hot furnace waste that burnt its last 200 or more years ago.

Artificial waterways were key to the great industrial revolution that transformed Britain and the world. The canals constituted a revolution in their own right. Beginning with the Sankey Canal and the much more ambitious Bridgewater Canal in the 1750s, they rapidly spread liquid tentacles around the UK. Freight transport, especially of coal and agricultural resources, had increased exponentially by the end of the century. But radical though they were in their effect, the canals still relied on horsepower to haul the barges. So where there were canals, there were also towpaths.

The oldest towpath is in fact Roman. It follows the Foss Dyke in Lincolnshire, an artificial waterway of the ancient world. The path along its banks is now designated as a 'leisure facility', a destiny that it shares with around 2,200 miles of eighteenth- and early nineteenth-century canal towpaths – 2,200 miles of interlinked footpaths added to the national network.

69

Britain's oldest artificial waterway, the Foss Dyke, Lincolnshire, photographed in 1875. This stretch of the canal has now been upgraded as a leisure facility, and the once waterlogged towpath can be walked in comfort.

The Thames and Severn Canal, in Gloucestershire, was closed to waterborne traffic in 1927, and the canal bed is now dry and overgrown. But the towpath remains in active use, providing a pedestrian route between England's two greatest rivers.

Unlike other footpaths, however, towpaths are not part of the King's Highway. They are part of the estate of a national charity, the Canal & River Trust, the successor to the many private companies that built and originally owned different canals. The trust is dedicated to public enjoyment of the waterways, including pedestrian recreation. Ramblers are only barred from the towpaths when maintenance work is underway.

Railway building mania replaced canal mania from the 1830s onwards, devastating freight traffic on the waterways and driving canal companies into bankruptcy. But after a century and a half of dominating transport, railways, too, faced a reckoning.

Nemesis came in the shape of Dr Richard Beeching, the technocrat brought in to rationalise the chaotic mass of tracks, many barely used, that had been spawned by railway mania.

The system was profuse with small, unprofitable, mostly rural lines; of richly scenic tracks plied by empty, doddery trains. Such a line was the Somerset & Dorset, beloved by railway enthusiasts but despised by those with serious travel needs, who dubbed it the 'slow and dirty'. Dr Beeching ripped up the S&D and other lines across the nation with the ruthless ferocity of a Viking yielding a battle-axe.

The Tramway Bridge over the river at Stratford-upon-Avon. Much used by tourists, it forms part of a footpath system that runs through the town along the track of the one-time Stratford and Moreton tramway. One of the world's first rail systems, the tramway was opened in 1826, some years before the advent of steam locomotives. It employed newly devised wrought-iron rails, but still depended on horse power to draw the wagons.

Not all axed lines were Beeching victims, however. A textbook case of a railway that was doomed before it even opened is the Mid Suffolk Light.[2] The line was already in receivership when it opened in 1904. Construction was never completed. The line just petered out and died in the middle of a field in the middle of nowhere. Yet, somehow it managed to soldier on as a working railway until final closure in 1952. Attracting the affection that the British habitually bestow on lost causes, the Mid Suffolk Light acquired the fond nickname 'the Middy'.

Much lamentation was bestowed on the closed railway lines, yet this was premature. Scores of them have lived on in a new way as footpaths and cycle tracks. The process began in 1979, when a group of volunteers led by John Grimshaw CBE rescued the abandoned Bristol and Bath railway track, renovating it for use by walkers and cyclists. The initiative burgeoned. Every county now has its share of one-time railway tracks, converted into footpath and cycleway use.

One of the railway names that now lives on is the Middy. Part of it has been restored as a visitor attraction with working trains. Much of the rest of the track has found a new lease of life as the Middy Railway Footpath. It has been claimed that the annual headcount of ramblers walking the path far exceeds the number of passengers who ever used the Middy in the days when it served as a mere railway.[3]

THE CANTERBURY & WHITSTABLE RAILWAY, 1830

A train on the Canterbury & Whitstable Railway approaches the sea down the steep incline from Blean Hill. Opened in 1830, and known lovingly as 'the Crab and Winkle', the line was the first passenger railway to open in the south of England. In common with hundreds of miles of other railway track across Britain, the stretch of track depicted in the picture now does service as a public footpath.

This imposing viaduct, built for the London & South Western Railway, straddles and dominates the Devonshire market town of Tavistock. Opened for traffic in 1859, the viaduct carried its last train in 1968.

Where locomotives once rumbled ... Like many other railway viaducts across Britain, the Tavistock Viaduct has now been downsized to function as a footpath and cycleway.

The end of the line for the locomotives of the Mid Suffolk Railway, now revived as a heritage railway.

Where the rails of the Mid Suffolk Light Railway end and the Middy Railway Footpath along the old track bed begins.

11

Fantasies and Science:
From Fairy Paths to Darwin

The footpath story is enlivened by many individual footpaths that have their own bizarre, mysterious or even dramatically significant tales to tell. What follows is just a sampling.

Fairy paths, touched on (cautiously) in the Introduction, are embedded in British folklore and many paths associated with this tradition can still be found around the British Isles, their sense of wild magic undiluted. In country districts, the belief in fairy paths lingered well into the late nineteenth century. The clergyman-diarist Francis Kilvert ran up against the old superstition in June 1871. It happened when he set out to spend the night on the top of Cader Idris, in the Snowdonia mountain group. Kilvert's guide, Old Pugh, refused to remain with him. 'It is said that if anyone spends a night alone on the top of Cader Idris he will be found either dead or a madman or a poet gifted with the highest degree of inspiration,' Kilvert wrote in his diary entry for 13 June 1871. 'Old Pugh says the fairies used to dance near the top of the mountain and he knows people who have seen them.'

Fairy paths were particularly associated with the approach to the ancient burial mounds known as long barrows.[1] Country people knew little of their origins, lost in the mists of time, but they did know that they were linked with the dead – and, in the words of the folklorist Katherine Briggs, 'the dead have been curiously entangled with fairies in popular tradition'.[2] One such mound, Fairy Toot, in Somerset, even owes its ancient name to the little folk.

In Cumbria, a fairy path has become a popular tourist attraction. The Fairy Steps at Beetham are a set of natural, but curiously regular steps, set in a cleft between two sheer rock faces. Local legend maintains that anybody who can climb the steps and squeeze through the gap without touching the sides will meet the fairies, and be granted a wish. Nobody thin enough to achieve this feat has, to date, been found, so the legend has yet to be put to the test. Adding to their slightly sinister aura, the steps formed part of a corpse road, the route by which coffins were carried from the surrounding countryside to the churchyard in the village of Beetham.

Tourists also head to a footpath in the village of Kilmersdon, Somerset, allegedly the inspiration for the path in the nursery rhyme 'Jack and Jill'.[3] Whether accurate or not, the

The Thames path, at Datchet, Berkshire. Footpaths are mentioned a number of times in the works of Shakespeare, but this one, referred to in *The Merry Wives of Windsor*, stands out as being a real, clearly identifiable path, largely unchanged since the Bard's time.

The Scots folk tale Thomas the Rhymer tells of a daredevil Scottish laird who took the forbidden fairy path up the Eildon Hills (see p. 8). At the summit, he was discovered, asleep, by the Queen of the Fairies. Thomas disappeared for seven years. When he finally re-emerged, he was clutching a fairy harp. He never again talked, but for the rest of his days communicated only in wild fairy song. (Painting, 1842, by Joseph Noel Paton)

The track to the peak of Cader Idris, in the Snowdonia National Park, was traditionally held by locals to be a fairy path. This image from the 1930s was taken on one of the rare days when the path was not shrouded by mist, adding to the sense of mystery and danger. (Raphael Tuck archive)

The approach to the hilltop West Kennet long barrow, Wiltshire. Myths swirled around these ancient burial places. The routes to them were regarded as 'fairy paths', the domain of the little people, never to be ventured on by night.

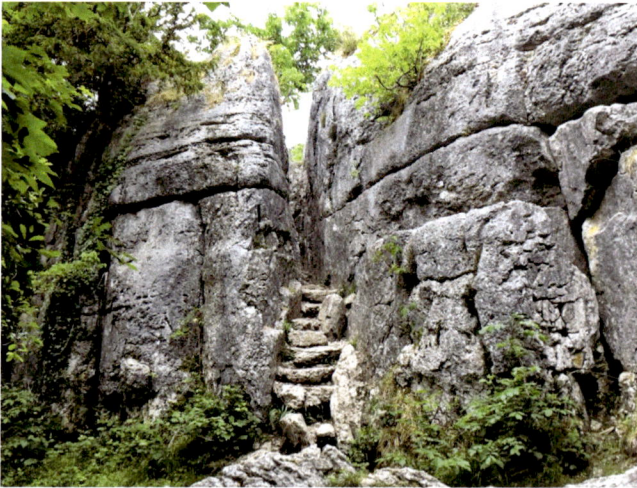

The Fairy Steps at Beetham, Cumbria. Anyone thin enough to squeeze up this flight of natural stone steps, without touching the sides, will be entitled to join the ranks of the fairies.

village has been trading off this association since the Victorian era. The story varies in detail, but the essence is that Jack and Jill were a young couple who lived together in the village. Such was their devotion that they fetched water together, a job normally given to the women and children of a household. Jack, who worked as a quarryman, was killed in a rock-fall. Jill died in childbirth, two days later. Different strands of this tragic tale were conflated into a Somersetshire country rhyme, which was picked up by the anthologist John Newbery, and first published as a nursery rhyme for children in 1795.

Britain, of course, heaves with ghosts, who share the national appetite for walking as a leisure activity, and apparently like little more than to take a night-time circuit around their old haunts. Mostly they tend to haunt such places as castle courtyards and the terraces of stately homes, but at least one ghost is associated with a country footpath.

Lady Alice Mildmay was the mistress of Great Graces, a Tudor manor house in Baddow, Essex. She was accustomed to take daily walks along the tree-lined avenue that leads

Above left: Perhaps Britain's most fabled footpath is the one that runs up Kilmersdon Hill, in Somerset. The path was the inspiration for the nursery rhyme Jack and Jill.

Above right: Lines from the nursery rhyme are inscribed on a series of markers alongside the path.

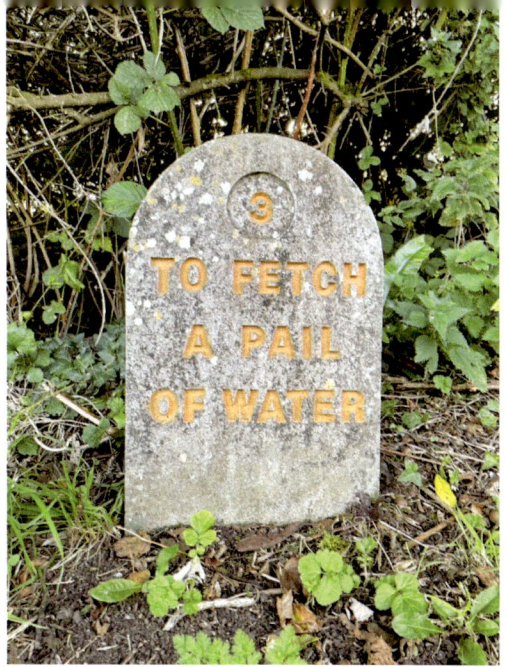

The famous well at the top of the hill, destination for the ill-fated couple.

Graces Walk, Baddow, Essex. The avenue footpath is said to be haunted by the sad ghost of Alice Mildmay.

through quiet countryside to the Tudor manor house where she lived. Then, one day in 1615, she jumped off the bridge which takes the avenue over the Sandon Brook. Her suicide was said to be the result of cruel treatment by her husband, Sir Henry Mildmay, though he himself was grief stricken by her death and himself died soon after.

Today, Great Graces is much reduced in size and grandeur, and the tree-lined avenue has dwindled into a mere public footpath. But Alice is said to continue her regular constitutionals up and down the old approach avenue. Whether this is true or fanciful, Graces Walk (as it is now known) remains a mecca for another type of otherworldly presence. Ghost hunters from far and wide are lured here. Specialists in the paranormal can be seen regularly cruising the walk, armed with twitching electronic antennae.

Fantasy and fable are one thing, but scientists also like to walk. Britain's two most famous naturalists, Gilbert White and Charles Darwin (one an accomplished amateur, the other a trained professional), share something in common, besides a lifetime's close-quarter study of living things. Both were path-makers.

Gilbert White spent his adult life as a curate in the village of Selborne, Hampshire. There, in 1720, he was born. There, in 1793, he would eventually be buried. In between, White walked and watched, seldom straying more than a mile or so from the vicinity of Selborne. But his achievements within this limited sphere were tremendous. He was the first to study intensively the ordinary birds and the little beasts of the British countryside. He did this with love, discipline and a commitment to the observation of living creatures, rather than specimens in a jar. He had no philosophical axe to grind, no thesis to support. He just set down things as they were.

The centre of White's field studies was 'the Hanger', a wooded hill above Selborne. The trees, mostly beech, did indeed hang as if for dear life on the hillside. In wet conditions, the Hanger could be positively dangerous to human life and limb.

To make the wood more accessible, White joined with his spendthrift brother John to cut the famous Zig-Zag up through Selborne Hanger. As its name (chosen by White himself) implies, the Zig-Zag was a footpath version of the hairpin-bend highways in the Alps. It was one of two enduring legacies bestowed on Selborne by its local hero. The other was White's

The famous Zig-Zag Path ascending Selborne Hanger in Hampshire. The path climbs the precipitate hillside in a series of twenty-seven zigs and zags, one of which is pictured.

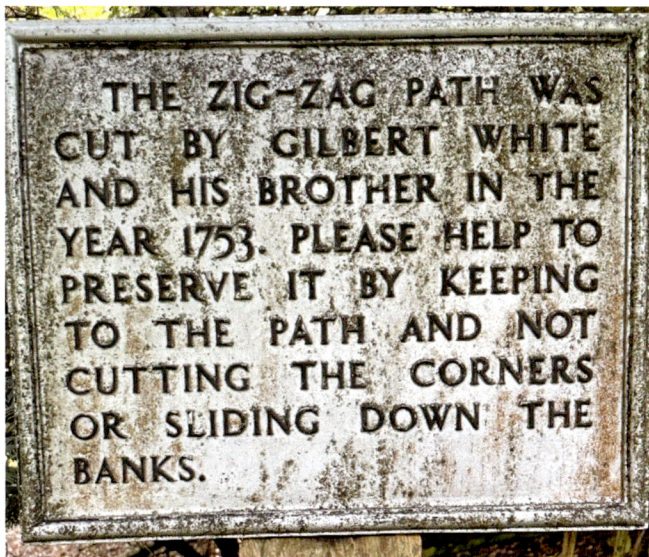

The final twist of the zig-zag revels this view over the village of Selborne and the Hampshire Downs beyond.

THE ZIG-ZAG PATH WAS CUT BY GILBERT WHITE AND HIS BROTHER IN THE YEAR 1753. PLEASE HELP TO PRESERVE IT BY KEEPING TO THE PATH AND NOT CUTTING THE CORNERS OR SLIDING DOWN THE BANKS.

A memorial at the base of the hanger, honouring Revd Gilbert White and his brother, the path's creators.

much-loved book *The Natural History of Selborne*. So many readers of the book arrived to walk the path that it was soon taken for granted as a right of way, and has remained so ever since.

White's admirers were legion, and one of them was Charles Darwin, whose ideas are among the most far-reaching and earth-shaking ever unleashed by a single human mind.[4] The Theory of Evolution resulted in Darwin entering the pantheon of the immortals within his own lifetime. But the man behind Evolution was never one for the limelight. He arrived back from his famous circumnavigation of the world aboard HMS *Beagle* and more or less hid in the shadows for the rest of his life. He might have created Darwinism, but he left it to other, more outgoing scientists, such as Thomas Huxley, to spread the word and engage in noisy brawls with bishops.

The retreat that Darwin chose was a country house on the Kent Downs. It was here that the Theory of Evolution itself evolved. It was teased into the open, slowly, and to an extent reluctantly (Darwin knew the explosive furore it would create). It emerged through a long process of both observation and dissection of specimens, but also through brooding. And Darwin did his thinking as he walked the lanes and footpaths around the village of Downe. Then, in 1846, Darwin constructed his own walk. It consisted of a quarter-mile stretch of path leading through a gate in the walled garden at Down House and along the edge of the adjoining meadow. In the corner of the meadow the great man planted a wood, with a choice of ways. On sunny days, Darwin could pace the south path. On colder days, when the wind blew in from the south-west, he would take the north route, his mighty brain sheltered from impudent gusts by the protecting trees.

It was the voyage on the *Beagle* and, in particular, Darwin's time in the Galapagos Islands that laid the foundations for the evolutionary hypothesis. But the theory was consolidated in the English countryside. On his walks, Darwin studied pigeons, bees and, in particular, earthworms. Somewhere out there in those chalk dells is Darwin's 'tangled bank', a complete ecosystem in miniature, 'clothed with plants of many kinds, with birds singing in the bushes, with various insects flitting about, and with worms crawling through the damp earth'. *The Origin of Species* ends with an encomium to the tangled bank.

The Sandwalk, Darwin's personal path, is the property of Down House, now managed by English Heritage as the Darwin museum. But it is bisected and accessed by an old public footpath. So walkers can follow in Darwinian footsteps, with the knowledge that this soil and these woods and meadows served to unlock so many of the great mysteries of life and creation.

Darwin's Sandwalk, the footpath laid down on his property by the author of *The Origin of Species*. Darwin could take a sheltered walk on either side of the small wood. His choice depended on the wind direction.

12

Gone to Town

The passage of time has seen the passing, even the vanishing, of entire settlements. A few ruts, hollows and mounds in a field can be the sole remnants of a once-great town or thriving village. But the one-time urban streets have tended to prove more resilient than buildings, and many survive as footpaths.

One particularly dramatic example can be found in Hampshire, where a public footpath follows a straight line of track across open pastoral country for just short of a mile. This track, along with a circlet of wall, is all that remains of the once-mighty Roman metropolis of Calleva (also known as Silchester).

The former high street of the Roman city Calleva survives as a farm track. Little else remains of the once-booming metropolis. This view is taken from Calleva's western entry point.

Calleva was a crossroads city of considerable significance. It presided over the meeting point of three major roads. The road known as the Devil's Highway ran from London to Exeter and Dorchester, the two great Roman strongholds in the West Country. When it reaches Calleva, it continues through the city's main gate and transforms into what we would now refer to as Calleva High Street or Calleva Broadway. With typically Roman precision, the highway exactly bisects the site of the old metropolis, dividing it into two equal-sized oval segments, defined by Calleva's outer walls and earth ramparts. Bang in the geometric centre of Calleva stood the main official buildings, forming a cluster on either side of the main street.

Unlike other metropolitan centres such as Canterbury, Colchester or York, Calleva did not survive the Roman departure from Britain in 410. It simply vanished into extinction. The inheritors of the land, the Saxon farmers and villagers of Hampton shire, had no interest in the decaying ruins, but the paved high street continued to remain useful as a thoroughfare. It survived as part of the farm track between the villages of Silchester and Stratfield Mortimer. When archaeologists began systematic investigation of the Calleva site in the 1860s, they were guided by the ancient trackway, which locals recognised as a right of way since time immemorial. Did they know that this was a right guaranteed by the highway laws of imperial Rome?

In Suffolk, another set of once-teeming urban streets have lapsed into rural decline to become just a range of pleasant country footpaths. Until the late thirteenth century, Dunwich was the east coast's answer to Bristol, a coastal port with a population and level of prosperity to rival any city in the land. Its wealth could be measured by the fact that it boasted nine fine churches. Dunwich families owned 'eighty great ships', and the harbour provided berthage to many more vessels, from all parts of Europe and beyond.

Then coastal erosion and a series of devastating storms destroyed its enormous harbour. The nine churches now lie beneath the North Sea. Having witnessed the devastating power of the sea at close quarters, Dunwich's surviving population fled, and settled inland, leaving their old hometown to the mercy of the waves and the shifting banks of shingle. In a short space of time, the once-mighty port became a ghost town. The site of its harbour can still be seen, and indeed, walked on, for it is now just a flat field.

In place of the imposing medieval port there is now an attractive, if slightly forlorn, cluster of cottages. They hug the ancient St James Street, old Dunwich's high street in everything but name. The nineteenth-century church of St James stands in for the nine magnificent churches lost to the sea. It is positioned at the site of a crossroads that was an axial point of the medieval city. To the north of the church, a path stretches out into the marshes, following the line of the one-time harbour rampart. At the point where St James Street meets St James' Church, the old high street continues its journey west from the shoreline, but now also as a footpath. As you follow the path, any remnants of once-proud Dunwich recede. Only the footpath, still following the line of the street, remains.

The UK has a number of vanished metropolitan sites. By contrast, the list of lost villages amounts to an estimated 3,000 or more.[1] They can be found in every county, indicated by an assortment of bumps and hollows, and, very often, a hollowed-out footpath that is the residue of a one-time village main street.

The forces that wiped villages off the map were various. The ravages of bubonic plague in the mid-fourteenth century often eliminated complete village populations. Such villages

The one-time high street of the vanished maritime city of Dunwich, in Suffolk. All significance gone, it has dwindled into a pleasant country footpath.

vanished without even the record of a name to commemorate them. The only memorial to their long-time existence is a footpath, once the community's main street. In other cases, a village population simply moved en masse to a better location (a case in point is Little Childerley in Cambridgeshire, where the inhabitants went to the trouble of dismantling their church and re-erecting it on the new site).

The most frequent cause was sheep. The great wool boom began in the mid-thirteenth century and soon grew to be the most lucrative commodity traded from the British Isles. Entire villages were razed to create extra grazing land. The sheep chomped the grass where once cottages had stood. Yet, in a now familiar story, the village streets survive in footpath form.

The complete sequence of village clearance and resultant wealth creation can be seen written into the land at Wormleighton, in Warwickshire. Here a footpath descends a hillside to the Oxford Canal. The route follows a hollow through the telltale grassy mounds and levelled rectangles of turf indicative of a one-time, now vanished, village settlement. The footpath, via the hollow, is following the line of Wormleighton's one-time village main street.

The village's residents were summarily evicted by the landlord, John Spencer, in 1499, and the land turned over to sheep. As usual, wool proved a much more lucrative cash crop

Old Wormleighton village, in Warwickshire, was levelled in 1499 to make way for sheep grazing. The only reminder of its existence is a series of grassy mounds, and what is now a footpath route, which follows the hollowed-out course of the village street. Sheep, perhaps descendants of the animals who ousted the original, human, inhabitants, continue to graze.

than the corn and oats that had preceded them. The Spencer family used the new wealth to construct a manor house, part of which still stands on top of the hill.

Landscape beautification rather than sheep accounted for the demise of Henderskelfe, in North Yorkshire. The village lay in what is now the landscape park of one of Britain's greatest country houses, Castle Howard. A turf walkway, lined with statues, leads from the south front of Castle Howard to the Temple of the Four Winds, designed, like the main house, by the great Sir John Vanbrugh. Unlike most turf walks of the era, which tended to be straight, this one follows a gentle curve, as it observes the line of Henderskelfe's vanished main street. Nothing, path apart, remains of Henderskelfe, whose inhabitants were relocated to the nearby village of Coneysthorpe.

Of course, the story of urbanisation has overwhelmingly been one of expansion, not oblivion. The cities and suburbs have marched across the land, engulfing rural areas. Observing this process, as London swelled and burst its bounds almost as he watched, the farmer and rural commentator William Cobbett compared the city to a great 'wen', or cyst, on the body of the land.

Yet, even the nineteenth-century capital of empire could be stopped in its tracks by a humble country footpath. Builders, laying bricks at a ferocious pace, had to tiptoe respectfully round these irritating little obstacles. Throughout London, there are places where ancient paths have been baked into the fabric of the city. Buildings surround them on either side, the tracks have been paved, but the old path routes remain, defiant. This chapter points to some examples of preserved pathways within the capital, but similar examples can be found in other great cities across the UK.

Known to all as 'The Hole in the Wall', this gap in a private wall allows pedestrian access between Rutland Gate and Rutland Street, in London's Knightsbridge area. The sole relic of an old country footpath, it survives as a right of way amid some of the most valuable residential real estate in Europe.

Lincoln's Inn Fields, the largest square in London, almost amounts to a museum of preserved country paths.[2] Its survival as a large open space results from the fact that it remained as farmland longer than any other segment of one-time London countryside. The great public square is accessed from the north by three alleyways: Great Turnstile, Little Turnstile and New Turnstile. Historically, these were stretches of path leading from the fields to the highway that became known as High Holborn. The turnstiles that give them their distinctive name were designed to give access to farm workers, while preventing the cattle from straying onto the streets of central London.

From the middle of the sixteenth century onward, buildings began to cluster alongside the paths. But vehicles never came this way. Great, Little and New Turnstiles have retained the pedestrian-only status enjoyed since time immemorial, although, with the loss of the original turnstiles, cows and sheep should find it easier to enter and exit.

Little Turnstile, London. This pedestrian alleyway, connecting Holborn to Lincoln's Inn Fields, follows the meanderings of a one-time rural footpath. The greenery is gone, replaced by paving and buildings, but the imprint of the old path remains, baked into the city's fabric.

On the outer edge of London lie a number of even doughtier survivors. A cross-hatching of old country footpaths exists just yards from the perimeter fence of Heathrow Airport. Millions of travellers come and go, every year, oblivious to the existence of these paths.

The site chosen for construction of the airport in the early 1950s was Hounslow Heath. The heath was regarded as 'barren'. Its low-fertility soil meant that it had never been systematically farmed, and was therefore dubbed 'of no value'.

But some scraps of the old heath survive as scrub, and, in one case, an old country house park adopted as a golf course. Many of the paths that criss-cross the heath were buried under concrete. But not all. Some co-exist alongside the great planes which take off and land from the world's second busiest international airport.

One of these paths has a particularly curious history. It curves south from the Grand Union Canal to a point where it is curbed abruptly by the M4 motorway. This was once a garden path, running through the now vanished Richings landscape park (surrounding a grand country establishment known as Percy Lodge). In 1747 the proprietor, Lord Hertford, set out to make an artificial path through his estate. The walk was designed to look as natural as possible, formed 'into the resemblance of a wild lane in the country'.[3] Ironically, it has now turned into the thing that it was designed to resemble, indistinguishable from the other, older footpaths across Hounslow Heath.

All the paths survive comfortably beneath the shadow of the great jets, taking off and landing at the airport. Given the proven resilience of Britain's footpaths, it is a fair bet which will endure the longest, airport or paths. The paths may well still be in place long after Heathrow Airport has reached the final departure gate.

Only way to travel: an old country footpath leads directly to the perimeter of London Heathrow Airport, visible on the far side of the meadow.

13

Past and Future

In the mid-twentieth century the footpath system began to tap a new source of extra mileage, propelled by a new notion – paths laid down purely for recreation. This went hand in glove with the campaign to open up the countryside to the great urban populations. The stand-off came to a head with the famous Kinder Scout mass trespass of 1935. This was not a footpath conflict, per se. Rather, it amounted to a broader bid to open up the high moors and peaks. But some of those who took part were members of the fledgling Ramblers

The start of the trail up Kinder Scout, in the Derbyshire Peak District, scene of the famous 1935 mass trespass.

Association, which has since campaigned tirelessly against footpath losses. Half a century later, it was to take on the rogue landowner Nicholas van Hoogstraten (see Chapter 8).

The RA's secretary Tom Stephenson was instrumental in the setting up of Britain's first official long-distance footpath, or national trail, the Pennine Way, opened in April 1965.

The process of stitching together a LDW could prove tortuous. The planner and author Christopher John Wright recalled the Herculean efforts to create the Pembrokeshire Coast Path, finally opened in 1970. It involved 'years of negotiation for the new rights of way needed to complete the line, and the construction of nearly 500 stiles and more than 100 footbridges'.[1] In some areas, bulldozers had to be employed on the precipitate cliffs in order to clear a way.

The ranks of foes have steadily fallen away. A new generation of landowners has come onside. A symbolic moment was reached in September 1989, when, at the instigation of Queen Elizabeth II (herself a keen walker), a new access path was opened up through the royal Sandringham estate in Norfolk. Other landowners fell in behind the monarch.[2]

A footpath overlooking the village of Corton Denham, Dorset, recently resurrected thanks to the Ramblers' (formerly Ramblers Association) Don't Lose Your Way campaign.

Meanwhile, traditional sources have continued to contribute to the growth of the footpath network. The Devil's Punchbowl section of the Portsmouth road, poised above a natural chasm, stood as a fine testimonial to eighteenth-century turnpike road engineers. But it also created a bottleneck and regular 3-mile tailback on the A3. In 2011 the road was diverted through a new dual-carriageway tunnel. The old turnpike was closed to traffic, and converted into a footpath and bridleway. Here as elsewhere the mighty motor road, for long the acme of planning, has given way to the oldest form of human transport.

A remarkable juxtaposition of ancient and modern can be found at Creswell Crags, a gorge on the Nottinghamshire–Derbyshire border. The limestone cliffs rise above a lake, and halfway up runs a line of caves. They are cavemen caves, first occupied around 60,000 years ago. Within those cavernous spaces can be found the most northerly examples

A section of the A3 London to Portsmouth trunk road, once notorious for its permanent traffic queues, photographed shortly after closure and replacement by a tunnel. Taken in August 2011.

The same stretch of road, now redeveloped as a footpath and bridleway, photographed in September 2020.

Ancient and modern: the M25 motorway, glimpsed from Stane Street, close to the junction of the two highways. One is ancient Roman, the other twentieth century. Previously mighty Stane Street has dwindled into a footpath. Does the same destiny one day await the M25?

Possibly the oldest identifiable footpaths in Britain are the ones leading up to the caves of Creswell Crags, on the western edge of Sherwood Forest. The more recent path in the foreground is the one-time B2002, now closed to all but foot traffic.

of cave art in Europe. Tracks beaten all those millennia ago, from the floor of the gorge to the mouths of the caves, may well be the oldest dateable footpaths in Britain.

Great tracts of time passed. Then, for a short-lived period, a new presence invaded the ancient gorge – traffic. It didn't take long before the vibration from motor vehicles on the Holdback to Worksop road began to threaten the very stability of the crags, to an extent not known since their formation in the Permian Age, 250-odd-million years ago. In 2006 the road was closed, and reclassified as a footpath. Yet another new recruit had been absorbed into the footpath system, and, once again, path power had triumphed.

The one-time B2002 runs at right angles to the ancient paths that climb to the Creswell caves. The ancient path and the decommissioned road now meet to form a line of T-junctions. The two arms of the junctions are separated by a 60,000-year gap, yet they share the same status and the same purpose. What better symbol could there be of the ever-evolving footpath system, carrying us not just to all points of the compass, but in both directions of time, pointing the way back into the past, and at the same time forward into whatever lies ahead and beyond.

Acknowledgements

Thanks to the estate of Denys Watkins-Pitchford and the BB Society for consent to publish the image on p. 15; to the Shell Archive for use of the paintings by David Gentleman, pp. 18, 25 and 48; to the late Captain Edward Clack for permission to use his aerial photograph of Pleshey, p. 32; to Ron Case, for the picture of the Broomway, p. 34; to Marsden History Group, for the image on p. 56.

All other images are either the author's photographs or in the public domain.

Notes

1. Introduction

1. Quoted in Richard Mabey, *Gilbert White: A Biography*, p. 26.
2. See Paul Clayton and John Trevelyan, *Rights of Way: A Guide to Law and Practice* (1983).
3. *Our Old Home*, Chapter (unnumbered) on Leamington Spa.
4. For use law relating to rights of way, see Ian Campbell, *A Practical Guide to the Law of Footpaths and Bridleways* (1974).
5. Robert Graves, *Goodbye to All That* (1929), Chapter 29.

2. Ancient Origins: Animal Tracks

1. T. E. Lawrence, *Seven Pillars of Wisdom* (1926), Chapter XLI. Back in England, Lawrence briefly lived alongside an ancient, possibly badger-forged, footpath at Pole Hill, Epping Forest.
2. Edward Thomas, 'The Combe' (poem, 1914).

3. Ancient Origins: Humans Stride Out

1. Alfred Watkins, *The Old Straight Track* (1925), Chapter 1.

4. Conflict and Colonisation

1. Information on Roman highway law and engineering standards is taken from Adolf Berger, *Encyclopaedic Dictionary of Roman Law* (1953).
2. Bill Bryson, *Notes from a Small Island* (1996), Chapter 14.

6. Paths in the Life of the Land

1. See A. K. Astbury, *Estuary: Land and Water in the Lower Thames Basin* (1980), Chapter 10.
2. See John M. Steane, *The Northamptonshire Landscape* (1974), pp. 50–51.
3. John Skinner, *Journal of a Somerset Rector 1803 to 1834*, entries for 11 June 1821 and 18 July 1828.
4. Thomas Tusser, *Five Hundred Points of Good Husbandry* (1562), Chapter 52, stanza 19.
5. 1948 BBC broadcast, collection of Christopher Somerville.

7. Boundaries

1. W. G. Hoskins, *Fieldwork in Local History* (1967), p. 142.
2. See Peter Hunter Blair, *Anglo-Saxon England* (1966), Chapter IV: 5.
3. Thomas Hardy, *Tess of the d'Urbervilles* (1891), Chapter XI.
4. Leslie W. Hopple and Alison M. Dogged, *The Chilterns* (1992), p. 34.
5. Shakespeare, *The Winter's Tale*, IV, iii, 119–22.

8. Path Wars

1. Material on the Battle of Leckhampton Hill draws closely on David Bick's account in *Old Leckhampton* (1994).
2. Report in *The Times*, 4 October 1989.
3. Report in *The Sunday Times*, 14 December 2002.

9. From Highway to Byway

1. Facts and figures in this section are taken from William Albert, *The Turnpike Road System in England 1663–1840* (1972).

10. Footprints of Industry

1. The ensuing paragraphs draw substantially on Ernest Straker, *Wealden Iron* (1931).
2. See Nicholas Comfort, *The Mid Suffolk Light Railway* (1997).
3. Information from Visit Suffolk.

11. Fantasy and Science: From Fairy Paths to Darwin

1. See Katherine Briggs (ed.), *Folklore, Myths and Legends of Britain* (1973), pp. 116–21.
2. Quoted in Paul Deveraux, *Fairy Paths & Spirit Roads* (2003), p. 48.

3. See Iona and Peter Opie, *The Oxford Dictionary of Nursery Rhymes* (1952).
4. See Richard Mabey, *Gilbert White: A Biography* (2021), p. 6.

12. Gone to Town

1. See Maurice Beresford, *Lost Villages of England* (1954).
2. See Ben Weinreb and Christopher Hibbert, *The London Encyclopaedia* (1993).
3. Quoted in Jane Brown, *The Omnipotent Magician: Lancelot 'Capability Brown'* (2011), p. 113.

13. Past and Future

1. Christopher John Wright, *A Guide to the Pembrokeshire Coast Path* (1986), Introduction.
2. Report in *The Times*, 13 September 1989.